STRATEGIES FOR SUCCESS

WRITING

Judith Andrews Green, Director
Oxford Hills Adult Community Education
South Paris, Maine

Susan D. McClanahan
Educational Consultant

Donna D. Amstutz
Special Advisor to the Series

STECK-VAUGHN ADULT EDUCATION ADVISORY COUNCIL

Meredyth A. Leahy
Director of Continuing Education
Cabrini College
Radnor, Pennsylvania

Roberta Pittman
Director, Project C3
Adult Basic Education
Detroit Public Schools
Detroit, Michigan

Jane B. Sellen
Supervisor, Adult Education
Western Iowa Tech Community College
Sioux City, Iowa

Don F. Seaman
Professor, Adult Education
College of Education
Texas A & M University
College Station, Texas

Elaine Shelton
Consultant, Competency-Based
Adult Education
Austin, Texas

Bobbie L. Walden
Coordinator, Community Education
Alabama Department of Education
Montgomery, Alabama

STECK-VAUGHN COMPANY
AUSTIN, TEXAS
A Division of National Education Corporation

Product Design and Development: McClanahan & Company

Project Director: Larry Anger

Design: Ellen Rongstad

Production: Carreiro Design

Editor: Karen Davy

Photo Research: Carrie Croton

ISBN 0-8114-1879-0

Acknowledgments

With thanks to Jeri Weaver for her contributions to the book and for writing the "Strategies for Success."

And to Kathryn Riley for her assistance with the section on Sentences.

Contents

To the Student

THIS BOOK AND THE GED TEST

The five sections of the GED Test measure what you know about science, mathematics, social studies, reading, and writing. This book covers one of those five areas, WRITING. There are four other books like this one. They cover the four other areas of study for the GED Test.

The WRITING part of the GED Test covers punctuation, capitalization, spelling, and grammar. It asks you to identify errors and recognize correct, well-written sentences. This book covers similar material.

This book is a good place to begin preparing for the GED Test. It gives you an idea of what the test will cover. And it gives you practice in taking tests.

STRATEGIES FOR SUCCESS

In each of the five books in this series, you will find sections called *Strategies for Success*. These sections in READING, SOCIAL STUDIES, and SCIENCE will help you increase your reading power. *Strategies for Success* in WRITING and MATHEMATICS will develop your critical thinking skills.

SELF-TESTS

A Self-Test follows each lesson. The Self-Tests are designed to help you find out what you have learned. There are practical writing exercises in the Self-Tests. Also, there are questions similar to those on the GED Test. They give you an idea of what the GED Test will be like.

ANSWERS AND EXPLANATIONS

The answer keys at the end of each unit will give you the best answer for each question. For many questions, the answer key will explain why one particular answer to a question is correct, and why the other answers are wrong. These explanations provide valuable test-taking tips.

LEARNING HOW TO LEARN

There are tricks to learning and remembering. Try out different ways of learning things. Find out what ways are best for you. Here are some tips that will help you get the most out of any studying you do or any test you take.

Keep a Notebook. Taking notes about what you are learning may be hard for you at first. You may think you can't do it, or that you can't spell. Don't worry about your spelling. Your notebook is your learning tool. No one has to see it but you. You'll be surprised how interesting rereading your notes at a later time will be. And you will be surprised at how much it will help you to remember. You will find that taking notes is another way of learning.

Hard Words. It isn't necessary to know every word to understand what you're reading. When you come to a hard word, don't stop. Keep on reading. The rest of the sentence or paragraph will probably help you figure out what the word means. In fact, people learn most new words that way. Use the Glossary at the end of the book to review the important words and concepts you have learned.

Understanding New Subjects. When anyone is learning about a new subject, understanding comes a little bit at a time. It's like putting the pieces of a puzzle together. When you run into something that is very hard, it is better to keep reading to the end of the paragraph or section. You can put question marks with your pencil by the parts you don't understand.

Later, reread the parts that gave you trouble. Some of the hard parts will start to make sense. Try to connect the information you are reading to the examples on the page. If you have a chance, talk over the hard parts with others. Don't think you have to understand everything the first time. IT'S OK TO REREAD.

Use the Study Aids in Your Book. Pay attention to what the table of contents, the unit titles, and the chapter titles can tell you about what you're reading. Also, there are explanations of important words in the margins of the pages. The pictures and illustrations often give clues about what you're learning. Be sure to look at them. All of these things will help you understand.

Use the Practice Questions to Learn. Study the answers and explanations to each question in the Self-Tests. This will help you understand the lessons you read and the information you learn.

Improve Your Test-Taking Skills. Many tests, including the GED Test, use multiple-choice questions. Each question is followed by five answers. You have to choose the BEST answer. Practice in taking tests like the ones in this book helps you to score higher on important tests like the GED.

Check What You Know

Check What You Know will give you an idea of the kind of work you will be doing in this book. It will give you an idea of your strengths in writing. And it will show you which writing skills you need to improve. These skills are important in passing tests like the GED Test.

Check What You Know is very similar to the WRITING part of the GED Test. There are 30 questions on this test.

Read each question carefully. Then put an X next to the BEST answer. There is no time limit.

CAPITALIZATION

Put an X next to the underlined part of the sentence that is NOT correct. If there is no error, mark number (5).

1. Did i tell you about the sale at Morgan's?
   _____ (1) Did
   _____ (2) i
   _____ (3) you
   _____ (4) Morgan's
   _____ (5) no error

2. Sometimes Easter is in march, and sometimes it's in April.
   _____ (1) Sometimes
   _____ (2) Easter
   _____ (3) march
   _____ (4) April
   _____ (5) no error

3. I recently read Alice Walker's novel, the Color Purple.
   _____ (1) novel
   _____ (2) the
   _____ (3) Color
   _____ (4) Purple
   _____ (5) no error

4. Out Of Africa was a best-selling book for several months.
   _____ (1) Out
   _____ (2) Of
   _____ (3) Africa
   _____ (4) months
   _____ (5) no error

PUNCTUATION

Put an X next to the underlined part of the sentence that is NOT correct. If there
is no error, mark number (5).

5. Are you and <u>your</u> wife interested in
   free <u>gifts</u> from <u>our</u> company<u>.</u>
   - ____ (1) your
   - ____ (2) gifts
   - ____ (3) our
   - ____ (4) .
   - ____ (5) no error

6. <u>Dont</u> forget <u>your</u> friends while <u>you're</u>
   away<u>.</u>
   - ____ (1) Dont
   - ____ (2) your
   - ____ (3) you're
   - ____ (4) .
   - ____ (5) no error

7. <u>She's</u> the most intelligent one in the
   class, but <u>her</u> grades <u>aren't</u> as high as
   <u>Marys'</u>.
   - ____ (1) She's
   - ____ (2) her
   - ____ (3) aren't
   - ____ (4) Marys'
   - ____ (5) no error

Put an X next to the sentence that is punctuated correctly.

8. ____ (1) I bought ham, cheese, peanut, butter, apple, jelly and
   bread.
   ____ (2) I bought ham, cheese, peanut, butter, apple jelly and
   bread.
   ____ (3) I bought ham cheese, peanut butter, apple jelly and bread.
   ____ (4) I bought ham, cheese, peanut butter, apple jelly and
   bread.
   ____ (5) All the sentences are punctuated incorrectly.

SENTENCES

Put an X next to the group of words that is NOT a correct and complete sentence. If all the sentences are correct, mark number (5).

9. ____ (1) The last month of the year.
____ (2) December has 31 days.
____ (3) December is the last month of the year.
____ (4) Christmas is in December.
____ (5) All are complete sentences.

10. ____ (1) He's as sly as a fox.
____ (2) A fox is a mammal.
____ (3) A crafty, sly, or clever person.
____ (4) The fox is related to the wolf.
____ (5) All are complete sentences.

11. ____ (1) Come on.
____ (2) Come with us.
____ (3) We thought you would be able to come with us tonight.
____ (4) We hope you'll come with us.
____ (5) All are complete sentences.

Put an X next to the best way to change each group of words into a complete sentence. Mark number (5) if no change is needed.

12. After we met for the first time.
____ (1) Add the words and talked for awhile.
____ (2) Add the words last month.
____ (3) Take away the word After.
____ (4) Take away the words the first time.
____ (5) No change is needed.

13. Before inviting her to dinner.
____ (1) Add the words he asked if she liked Chinese food.
____ (2) Add the words he asked if she liked.
____ (3) Take away the word Before.
____ (4) Take away the words to dinner.
____ (5) No change is needed.

NOUNS, PRONOUNS, AND ADJECTIVES

Four words are underlined in each of the following sentences. If an error is underlined, put an X next to the number. If there is no error, mark number (5).

14. Ladies and gentlemen, you have helped our childs by being aware of these problems.
    - _____ (1) Ladies
    - _____ (2) gentlemen
    - _____ (3) childs
    - _____ (4) problems
    - _____ (5) no error

15. We all have our own lifes to live in our own ways.
    - _____ (1) We
    - _____ (2) our
    - _____ (3) lifes
    - _____ (4) ways
    - _____ (5) no error

16. She and him have been going together since their first date two years ago.
    - _____ (1) She
    - _____ (2) him
    - _____ (3) together
    - _____ (4) their
    - _____ (5) no error

17. We don't think it will take us too long to find them.
    - _____ (1) We
    - _____ (2) it
    - _____ (3) us
    - _____ (4) them
    - _____ (5) no error

18. It was a happy occasion; the bride and groom were radiantly.
    - _____ (1) happy
    - _____ (2) bride
    - _____ (3) groom
    - _____ (4) radiantly
    - _____ (5) no error

19. Thank you for your kind and newsy letter.
    - _____ (1) your
    - _____ (2) kind
    - _____ (3) newsy
    - _____ (4) letter
    - _____ (5) no error

VERBS AND ADVERBS

Four words or phrases are underlined in each of the following sentences. If an error is underlined, put an X next to the number. If there is no error, mark number (5).

20. Walter <u>try</u> to <u>call</u> you last night, but there <u>was</u> no <u>answer</u>.
    - _____ (1) try
    - _____ (2) call
    - _____ (3) was
    - _____ (4) answer
    - _____ (5) no error

21. <u>Do</u> you <u>know</u> why they <u>haven't</u> <u>arrived</u> yet?
    - _____ (1) Do
    - _____ (2) know
    - _____ (3) haven't
    - _____ (4) arrived
    - _____ (5) no error

22. Natalie <u>should</u> <u>tell</u> Jeremy the truth <u>quick</u> before <u>it's</u> too late.
    - _____ (1) should
    - _____ (2) tell
    - _____ (3) quick
    - _____ (4) it's
    - _____ (5) no error

23. He has been <u>hoping</u> to <u>get</u> a job since last May when he <u>was</u> <u>suddenly</u> fired.
    - _____ (1) hoping
    - _____ (2) get
    - _____ (3) was
    - _____ (4) suddenly
    - _____ (5) no error

24. <u>Neither</u> the police officer <u>nor</u> the old lady <u>remember</u> what <u>happened</u>.
    - _____ (1) Neither
    - _____ (2) nor
    - _____ (3) remember
    - _____ (4) happened
    - _____ (5) no error

25. <u>Not only</u> Plato <u>but also</u> Aristotle <u>was</u> a <u>famous</u> Greek philosopher.
    - _____ (1) Not only
    - _____ (2) but also
    - _____ (3) was
    - _____ (4) famous
    - _____ (5) no error

SPELLING

In each set of words, put an X next to the misspelled word. If there is no misspelled word, mark number (5).

26. _____ (1) describe
    _____ (2) noticeable
    _____ (3) judge
    _____ (4) develope
    _____ (5) no error

27. _____ (1) height
    _____ (2) weight
    _____ (3) neice
    _____ (4) receive
    _____ (5) no error

28. _____ (1) occurring
    _____ (2) reccommendation
    _____ (3) arrangement
    _____ (4) written
    _____ (5) no error

29. _____ (1) unconscious
    _____ (2) seperate
    _____ (3) supervisor
    _____ (4) committee
    _____ (5) no error

30. _____ (1) bicycle
    _____ (2) icycle
    _____ (3) emphasize
    _____ (4) familiar
    _____ (5) no error

When you finish the test, compare your answers with those in *Answers and Explanations* on page 8. Then complete the chart on page 7 by checking the numbers of the questions you got wrong.

SKILL PREVIEW CHART

The chart will show you which writing skills you need to pay special attention to. Reread each question you got wrong. Then look at the appropriate sections of the book for help in figuring out the right answers.

SKILLS	TEST QUESTIONS	STRATEGIES FOR SUCCESS
The test, like this book, focuses on the skills below.	Check (✔) the questions you got wrong.	Preview what you will learn in this book. Learn how to get the right answers.
Capitalizing Correctly	___ 1 ___ 3 ___ 2 ___ 4	See pages 22–23 STRATEGIES FOR SUCCESS ● Knowing What to Capitalize ● Knowing What NOT to Capitalize
Using Correct Punctuation	___ 5 ___ 7 ___ 6 ___ 8	See pages 40–41 STRATEGIES FOR SUCCESS ● Knowing Where to Punctuate
Writing Clear Sentences	___ 9 ___ 12 ___ 10 ___ 13 ___ 11	See pages 60–61 STRATEGIES FOR SUCCESS ● Writing Clear Sentences ● Correcting Non-Sentences
Using Appropriate Nouns, Pronouns, and Adjectives	___ 14 ___ 17 ___ 15 ___ 18 ___ 16 ___ 19	See pages 80–81 STRATEGIES FOR SUCCESS ● Using Pronouns Instead of Nouns ● Knowing When to Add Adjectives
Using Appropriate Verbs and Adverbs	___ 20 ___ 23 ___ 21 ___ 24 ___ 22 ___ 25	See pages 102–103 STRATEGIES FOR SUCCESS ● Using the Right Verb Form ● Adding Words to Describe Actions
Using Correct Spelling	___ 26 ___ 29 ___ 27 ___ 30 ___ 28	See pages 122–123 STRATEGIES FOR SUCCESS ● Spotting Spelling Problems ● Using the Dictionary

Answers and Explanations

CAPITALIZATION

1. (2) Always capitalize the word *I*.
2. (3) Always capitalize months of the year.
3. (2) Always capitalize the first word in a title.
4. (2) Small words such as *of* and *the* in the middle of titles are not capitalized.

PUNCTUATION

5. (4) Always put a question mark at the end of a question.
6. (1) *Don't* is an abbreviation for *do not* and needs an apostrophe to take the place of the missing letter.
7. (4) The apostrophe should come before the *s*.
8. (4) Peanut butter and apple jelly are single items.

SENTENCES

9. (1) There is no predicate in this group of words.
10. (3) There is no predicate.
11. (5) All are complete sentences.
12. (3) When you take away <u>After</u>, you have a complete idea.
13. (1) A complete idea is added to the phrase.

NOUNS, PRONOUNS, AND ADJECTIVES

14. (3) The correct plural is *children*.
15. (3) The correct plural is *lives*.
16. (2) The correct pronoun is *he*.
17. (1) There is no error.
18. (4) *Radiantly* is an adverb. Use the adjective *radiant* to describe nouns (bride and groom).
19. (5) There is no error.

VERBS AND ADVERBS

20. (1) Use the past tense *tried* when you write about what happened last night.
21. (5) There is no error.
22. (3) Use the adverb *quickly* to describe the verb *tell*.
23. (5) There is no error.
24. (3) Use *remember<u>s</u>* to match the second part of the compound subject (lady).
25. (5) There is no error.

SPELLING

26. (4) The correct spelling is <u>develop</u>.
27. (3) The correct spelling is <u>niece</u>.
28. (2) The correct spelling is <u>recommendation</u>.
29. (2) The correct spelling is <u>separate</u>.
30. (2) The correct spelling is <u>icicle</u>.

CAPITALIZING CORRECTLY

CAPITAL letters (ABC) attract more attention than small letters (abc).

Sometimes, ALL THE LETTERS in a word will be capitalized. You might see this done in ads and headlines. It gets your attention.

More often, only the first letter in a word is capitalized. Some examples of initial capitalization are Mrs. Joyce Jefferson, July 14, and Houston, Texas. This kind of capitalization and the kind at the beginning of sentences are covered in this unit.

1. SENTENCES

When do you **capitalize** the first letter of a word? **Specific** rules of grammar tell you when.

Capitalization is like a **code** between the writer and reader. It shows the reader which words begin sentences and which words are specific names of things.

The note below is difficult to follow because the writer ignored two basic rules:

1. Always begin a sentence with a capital letter.
2. The word *I* is always a capital letter.

Read the note. Circle the letters that need to be capitalized.

```
i don't care what you say.  a person can take
only so much.  it's easy for you to tell me
what to do.  you don't have to work there.
if you think i have it easy, you're wrong.
i'm ready to quit.
```

In correcting the note, you applied the two easy and important rules about capitalization. There are seven words that need to be capitalized: I, A, It's, You, If, I, I'm. The correct note should look like this:

```
I don't care what you say.  A person can take
only so much.  It's easy for you to tell me
what to do.  You don't have to work there.
If you think I have it easy, you're wrong.
I'm ready to quit.
```

CAPITALIZE. To begin with a capital letter.

SPECIFIC. Exact, definite.

CODE. A system of signals.

Some writers don't understand the rules of capitalization. They tend to overdo it. They start every word they think is important with a capital letter. The result is something like this:

Happy Holidays!
This has been a Great Year for Us! We were glad to get to see you all at the Beach this Past Summer. It was fun for the Kids too. Harry was Promoted last Month, so we may be taking even more Nice Vacations. Hope You Are All Well.
Love,
Winnie

In the note above, many of the capitalizations are correct. The **greeting** (Happy Holidays!) and **closing** (Love) are capitalized correctly. And the first letter in each sentence is capitalized. Of course, it is also correct to capitalize the first letter of the names of people (Harry). But there are 15 more words in the note that shouldn't be capitalized. Reread the note and circle the letters that should NOT be capitalized.

When you write, don't capitalize just to **emphasize** something. The following 15 words shouldn't be capitalized in the note above: great, year, us, beach, past, summer, kids, promoted, month, nice, vacations, you, are, all, well.

GREETING. A phrase that begins a letter.

CLOSING. A phrase that ends a letter.

EMPHASIZE. To make important.

Any kind of writing that you do will be clearer if you follow the rules of capitalization. These rules help you show the reader which words begin new sentences and which words are specific names of things. As you read the other chapters in this unit, you will notice that most names, dates, days, and places are capitalized.

*F*OR YOUR INFORMATION

Use of Capitalization in Titles

When you mention a specific title—of a book, record, movie, or TV show—how do you know which words to capitalize? Keep in mind these two rules:

1. The first and last words of a title are always capitalized.
2. All other words, except minor words like *of, and, to, for,* and *the,* are capitalized.

Here are some examples to help you remember these rules:

Every afternoon, she watches "The Young and the Restless" and "As the World Turns."

Norman Mailer's first novel was *The Naked and the Dead.*

Some of the most popular movies of the past are *Gone with the Wind, The Sound of Music,* and *Close Encounters of the Third Kind.*

$\mathcal{S}$*elf-Test*

Answer the questions. Then compare your answers with those in *Answers and Explanations* **on page 24.**

Each sentence below has one mistake in capitalization. Rewrite the sentences and correct the mistakes.

1. I tried my best, but i didn't make it.

   _____

   _____

2. there aren't any good movies on tonight.

   _____

   _____

3. i told you to be more careful.

   _____

   _____

4. Wilma told me You called.

   _____

   _____

5. Your horoscope says that Friends will be important today.

   _____

   _____

6. Do you feel Better now?

   _____

   _____

7. She asked me if i ever get tired of baby-sitting.

   _____

   _____

8. we should try that new Cuban restaurant on the corner.

   _____

   _____

2. DAYS AND DATES

All the months of the year begin with a capital letter: January, February, March, April, May, June, July, August, September, October, November, December.

September						
Sunday	Monday	Tuesday	Wednesday	Thursday	Friday	Saturday

But the seasons aren't capitalized: spring, summer, autumn (fall), winter.

All the days of the week begin with a capital letter: Sunday, Monday, Tuesday, Wednesday, Thursday, Friday, Saturday.

All the names of specific holidays begin with a capital letter too, for example, Halloween, Thanksgiving Day, New Year's Eve, Yom Kippur, and Christmas Day.

But words such as *today*, *tomorrow*, and *yesterday* aren't capitalized.

Apply the rules of capitalization and answer the following questions. Write complete sentences.

1. What is today's date?

_____

2. What day of the week is this?

_____

3. What holiday is nearest to today's date?

_____

4. What is your favorite season and why?

_____

Here are some sample answers to the questions on the preceding page.

1. Today is March 20, 1987.
2. This is Friday.
3. The holiday nearest to today's date is Easter.
4. My favorite season is winter because I look forward to Thanksgiving Day, Christmas Day, and New Year's Eve.

FOR YOUR INFORMATION

When you write days and dates, always put them in this order, with the day first:

Sunday, March 5, 1988

If you use abbreviations, the same date looks like this:

Sun., Mar. 5, 1988

To make dates even shorter, you can write them all as numbers. Each set of numbers is separated by a slash mark. March is the third month of the year. Write only the last two numbers of the year.

3/5/88

Sometimes, on an application form, you might see a set of boxes like this:

Date of Birth:

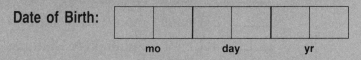

If your birthday were April 2, 1959, you would fill in the blanks like this:

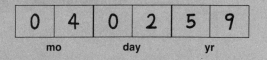

Self-Test

Put an X next to the best way to correct each sentence.

1. This year Thanksgiving day comes on Thursday, November 26.
   - ＿＿＿ (1) Change day to Day.
   - ＿＿＿ (2) Change Thursday to thursday.
   - ＿＿＿ (3) Change November to november.
   - ＿＿＿ (4) Change year to Year.
   - ＿＿＿ (5) No change is needed.

2. Christmas Eve is always on December 24, the day before Christmas.
   - ＿＿＿ (1) Change Eve to eve.
   - ＿＿＿ (2) Change December to december.
   - ＿＿＿ (3) Change day to Day.
   - ＿＿＿ (4) Change Christmas to christmas.
   - ＿＿＿ (5) No change is needed.

3. Enid told me Yesterday that she and Bob plan to get married this summer, probably in August.
   - ＿＿＿ (1) Change Yesterday to yesterday.
   - ＿＿＿ (2) Change she to She.
   - ＿＿＿ (3) Change summer to Summer.
   - ＿＿＿ (4) Change August to august.
   - ＿＿＿ (5) No change is needed.

4. The parade was on Columbus Day, a Monday, not on october 18, a Sunday.
   - ＿＿＿ (1) Change Day to day.
   - ＿＿＿ (2) Change parade to Parade.
   - ＿＿＿ (3) Change Sunday to sunday.
   - ＿＿＿ (4) Change october to October.
   - ＿＿＿ (5) No change is needed.

5. She turned 40 on her Birthday, February 14, which was also Valentine's day.
   - ＿＿＿ (1) Change Birthday to birthday and day to Day.
   - ＿＿＿ (2) Change Birthday to birthday and February to february.
   - ＿＿＿ (3) Change February to february and day to Day.
   - ＿＿＿ (4) Change Valentine's to valentine's and day to Day.
   - ＿＿＿ (5) No change is needed.

6. According to the almanac, July is usually the hottest month of the Summer.
   - ＿＿＿ (1) Change July to july.
   - ＿＿＿ (2) Change month to Month.
   - ＿＿＿ (3) Change Summer to summer.
   - ＿＿＿ (4) Change month to Month and Summer to summer.
   - ＿＿＿ (5) No change is needed.

3. PEOPLE AND PLACES

People's names always begin with capital letters. Use capital letters for their first, middle, and last names. Use capital letters for their initials too. If a man's name includes the word *Junior*, that is also capitalized.

John F. Kennedy

Susan B. Anthony

Dr. Martin Luther King, Jr.

Titles like *Mr.*, *Mrs.*, *Ms.*, and *Miss* are always capitalized. If a title like *Doctor* or *Reverend* is included with the person's name, that is also capitalized.

Miss Myrtle Clark	Dr. José Alvarez	Mr. Larry Young
Rev. Darrel Berg	Mrs. Joan L. Pauley	Ms. Mary Lin

Sometimes at work you are asked to give information that can be used in case of an emergency. Write the names of a close relative or friend and your doctor in the blanks below:

Person to be notified
in case of emergency: _____
Personal physician: _____

Did you remember to include full names and titles? Your names should look something like these:

Joan L. Pauley   Dr. José Alvarez

If you call someone by a title, you capitalize the title just as you would capitalize a name. For example, you would say, "Hello, Doctor. Am I late?" just as you would say, "Hello, Frank. Am I late?" The word *Doctor* takes the place of a name, so it is capitalized.

But you do NOT capitalize if you are using the title to describe someone's job or a person's **relationship** to you. For example:

I should make an appointment with my doctor.

Here, the word *doctor* isn't a substitute for a person's name. So the word *doctor* shouldn't be capitalized.

Most of the words in an address begin with a capital letter. The name of a street is capitalized, and so are the words *Street*, *Drive*, *Road*, and *Avenue* when they follow the name.

Mrs. Judy Myers
3001 Lexington Road
Baltimore, MD 20018

Mr. and Mrs. Jerry McCord
1800 Marshall Street
Lincoln, NE 68505

Every city, state, county, and country begins with a capital letter. Look at these examples:

They moved from Billings, Montana to Waycross, Georgia last year.
The schools in Montgomery County are excellent.
They came to the United States from the Republic of South Africa.

Notice that the word *the* isn't capitalized when it's part of the name of a country—the United States, the Republic of South Africa.

Every state has a two-letter abbreviation. Both letters are capitalized. The two-letter abbreviation is usually used when addressing letters. It is also correct to write out the state or to abbreviate it in another way.

San Antonio, TX OR San Antonio, Texas
Watertown, MA OR Watertown, Mass.

Address this envelope to a friend. Include your full **return address** in the upper left corner. Use the two-letter abbreviations for the states in the addresses.

You should also capitalize the names of specific rivers, lakes, bays, parks, mountain ranges, and buildings. For example, you would write:

We saw the Colorado River and the Rocky Mountains.

But the words *river, bay, lake, mountain,* and *building* aren't capitalized if they aren't part of the name of a specific place.

We saw the river and the mountains.

Write a sentence about a specific place (river, lake, bay, park, mountain, or building) you've visited in your state.

_____

_____

Write the same sentence without naming the place by its specific title.

_____

_____

Your sentences should look something like these:

We visited the Empire State Building.
We visited a tall building.

RETURN ADDRESS.
The address a letter comes from.

Lake Champlain

the Rocky Mountains

the Empire State Building

Self-Test

Answer the questions. Then compare your answers with those in *Answers and Explanations* on page 25.

Each sentence below has one or two mistakes in capitalization. Rewrite the sentences and correct the mistakes.

1. You really need to see a Doctor, Sister.

   _____

   _____

2. I recommended Dr. Robert P. Wong to my Mother.

   _____

   _____

   _____

3. Mr. Martínez met miss Foster and her Son for a quick cup of coffee.

   _____

   _____

4. Send the bill to ms. Marilyn Stuart, 6701 Lincoln street, Portland, ME.

   _____

   _____

   _____

5. The White House and the Washington monument are two Buildings that tourists love to visit.

   _____

   _____

   _____

6. On their trip to the western States, Mr. and Mrs. Mitzner saw the Grand Canyon, Yellowstone National park, and two state parks.

   _____

   _____

   _____

   _____

_T_HINKING AND WRITING

1. Use the rules of capitalization to complete the form below. Your name should include your title (Mr., Ms., etc.) and your middle name or initial if you use it. The address should be complete. Write the correct two-letter abbreviation for the state.

83¢ AN ISSUE

Send me the next 12 issues (1 year) of _Consumer World_ for the low basic rate of $9.95. That's 58% off the single copy price.

NAME _____

ADDRESS _____

CITY _____ STATE _____ ZIP _____

☐ **Bill me later**   ☐ **Payment enclosed**

---

2. Write a sentence about a teacher, doctor, or minister you admire. Include that person's full name and title in your sentence.

_____

_____

_____

3. Write two or three sentences telling about a specific place you'd like to visit or return to.

_____

_____

_____

_____

Compare your answers with those in _Answers and Explanations_ on page 26.

STRATEGIES FOR SUCCESS

1. KNOWING WHAT TO CAPITALIZE

It's important to know which words to capitalize. It makes your writing clearer.

STRATEGY: Train your eyes to look for key words.

1. Look for *I* and look for names.
2. Notice where sentences start.

Example: Which words in the following passage should be capitalized?

> i've decided i should return to texas, where job opportunities are better. my wife, barbara, agrees. we will be happier there than we have been in kansas.

I and words with *I* (I've) should be capitalized. Texas and Kansas are names of states, and Barbara is a person's name. They are all capitalized. Two sentences besides the one with *I* should be capitalized too. They begin with *My* and *We*.

Write: Rewrite these two sentences, capitalizing correctly.

i come from the lipari islands, a group of islands off the coast of italy. They are also known as the aeolian islands.

_____

_____

_____

_____

KANSAS

TEXAS

2. KNOWING WHAT NOT TO CAPITALIZE

Sometimes it isn't correct to capitalize a word.

STRATEGY: Always reread what you write.

Words that are not specific names of people, places, or things should not be capitalized.

Example: Which words in this paragraph should NOT be capitalized?

The Salton Sea is a shallow Salt Lake about 300 square miles in area. It is located in California. It was formed by the flooding of the Colorado River. The River flooded around the Year 1905.

In this context, *salt lake* is not a specific lake. *River* and *year* are not part of specific names in the last sentence. None of these words should be capitalized.

Write: Rewrite this paragraph with correct capitalization.

during the 1930s, a Woman named Mary mallon worked as a cook. She had come to the united states from ireland many years before. several people who ate what she cooked became ill and died. It was soon discovered that She was a typhoid carrier, and was giving the disease to everyone. This caused her to be nicknamed typhoid mary.

_____

_____

_____

_____

_____

_____

_____

_____

Compare your answers with those in *Answers and Explanations* on page 26.

Answers and Explanations

1. SENTENCES

The mistakes in these sentences are corrected by following one of these three rules:

1. Begin every sentence with a capital letter.
2. The word *I* is always capitalized.
3. Avoid capitalizing words just because they seem important.

1. I tried my best, but I didn't make it.
2. There aren't any good movies on tonight.
3. I told you to be more careful.
4. Wilma told me you called.
5. Your horoscope says that friends will be important today.
6. Do you feel better now?
7. She asked me if I ever get tired of baby-sitting.
8. We should try that new Cuban restaurant on the corner.

2. DAYS AND DATES

1. (1) is the correct answer. Here, the word *Day* is part of the holiday name. Days of the week (Thursday) and months (November) are always capitalized. The word *year* isn't.

2. (5) *Eve* is part of the holiday name, but in this sentence *day* isn't. Months (December) and holidays (Christmas) are always capitalized.

3. (1) The word *yesterday* shouldn't be capitalized. There is no need to capitalize *she* or *summer*. Months (August) are always capitalized.

4. (4) *October* should be capitalized. *Day* is part of the holiday name. There is no need to capitalize *week*. Days of the week (Sunday) are always capitalized.

5. (1) The word *birthday* shouldn't be capitalized, but *Day* should be. Months (February) and holidays (Valentine's Day) are always capitalized.

6. (3) The word *summer* shouldn't be capitalized. Months (July) are always capitalized, but the word *month* isn't.

3. PEOPLE AND PLACES

1. You really need to see a doctor, Sister.

   The word *doctor* isn't a name substitute, but the word *Sister* is.

2. I recommended Dr. Robert P. Wong to my mother.

3. Mr. Martínez met Miss Foster and her son for a quick cup of coffee.

   Titles (Miss) are always capitalized. The word *son* isn't a name substitute in this sentence.

4. Send the bill to Ms. Marilyn Stuart, 6701 Lincoln Street, Portland, ME.

   Titles (Ms.) are capitalized, and so are words like *Street* when they are in an address.

5. The White House and the Washington Monument are two buildings that tourists love to visit.

   Specific buildings (Washington Monument) should be capitalized, but elsewhere the word *building* shouldn't be.

6. On their trip to the western states, Mr. and Mrs. Mitzner saw the Grand Canyon, Yellowstone National Park, and two state parks.

   The word *states* and the term *state parks* are not specific and shouldn't be capitalized. Yellowstone National Park is a name of a specific place, and each word should be capitalized.

THINKING AND WRITING

There are many ways to answer the questions. Here are some examples.

1.

83¢ AN ISSUE

Send me the next 12 issues (1 year) of *Consumer World* for the low basic rate of $9.95. That's 58% off the single copy price.

NAME *Mrs. Talia E. Gonzalez*

ADDRESS *5708 Medford Drive*

CITY *San Antonio*   STATE *TX*   ZIP *78209*

☒ **Bill me later**   ☐ **Payment enclosed**

---

2. I admire Rev. Mark L. McGinnis because he preaches sermons that people of all ages understand.

3. I would like to return to the Black Hills in South Dakota. We were there when I was little, and I still remember it.

STRATEGIES FOR SUCCESS

1. Knowing What to Capitalize

I come from the Lipari Islands, a group of islands off the coast of Italy. They are also known as the Aeolian Islands.

2. Knowing What NOT to Capitalize

During the 1930s, a woman named Mary Mallon worked as a cook. She had come to the United States from Ireland many years before. Several people who ate what she cooked became ill and died. It was soon discovered that she was a typhoid carrier, and was giving the disease to everyone. This caused her to be nicknamed Typhoid Mary.

USING PUNCTUATION

WHEN you read, you can't "hear" the writer's voice. So writers use punctuation to tell you when they're asking questions, when they want you to stop or pause, or when they're excited about something. Punctuation gives you information beyond what the words say.

Punctuation is a set of symbols called punctuation marks. Some common punctuation marks are the period (.), the question mark (?), the exclamation point (!), quotation marks ("..."), the comma (,), and the apostrophe (').

1. SENTENCE ENDINGS

A sentence always begins with a capital letter. A sentence always ends with some kind of **punctuation**. This can be a period, question mark, or exclamation point.

The ending mark you will use most is the period. It is used for regular sentences that give information and **state** facts. Most sentences in this book end with periods.

The second ending mark is the question mark. It shows the reader that the sentence is a question. A question means a person expects an answer.

Some questions can be answered with a "yes" or "no." These questions often begin with words such as *Are, Is, Do, Does, Did, Have, Will,* etc. For example:

Will you have time to help me after work?

Other questions need longer answers. These questions begin with *Who, What, Where, When, Why,* and *How.* For example:

What are you going to do after work?

The third ending mark is the exclamation point. It shows excitement. Think about what happens when you are excited about something—or scared or angry. A word or a very short sentence might just burst out of you. These are examples of **exclamations**:

Help!
Watch out!
Wow!
That's great!
Get out of my way!

From the **content** of these sentences, can you tell whether each one is a statement, a question, or an exclamation? Add correct punctuation to each sentence.

CONTENT. The subject, idea, or words.

What is psychology

Does it have something to do with people

Is it a science

How does it work

Psychology is the study of how people think and act

I knew that

You did

Wow

You're really smart

You probably found that once you added punctuation, the meaning of each sentence became more specific and clearer. You were correct if you added question marks to the first four sentences, periods to the next two, a question mark to the next sentence, and exclamation points to the last two sentences.

Now look at this birthday greeting.

Happy Birthday
Did you get the job We hope so
We look forward to seeing you
Frank and the kids next month at Mom's
It will be great to be together again
Take care   Love
                    Sally

Rewrite the above message, adding punctuation where you think it is needed.

_____

_____

_____

_____

_____

_____

Along with capitalization, punctuation is a kind of code between the writer and the reader. A writer uses punctuation to "talk" to the reader. Without it, the words alone are hard to follow. This is especially true when you read groups of sentences, as in the birthday greeting on the previous page.

Without punctuation, you don't know where to **pause** or what to emphasize in the birthday greeting. But look at the difference when punctuation is added. You can almost hear the writer talking to you.

PAUSE. To stop briefly.

Happy Birthday!
Did you get the job? We hope so.
We look forward to seeing you, Frank and the kids next month at Mom's. It will be great to be together again.
Take care.　　　Love,
　　　　　　　　Sally

FOR YOUR INFORMATION

The Colon

You may have noticed the colon (:) in this book. When you see a colon, it usually means that a set of examples or a list will follow. The colon is often used after phrases like *for example* and *as follows*.

A colon is one way the writer can list facts or ideas. A colon tells the reader to be on the lookout for some specific information or examples.

Self-Test

Answer the questions. Then compare your answers with those in *Answers and Explanations* on page 42.

Add periods, question marks, or exclamation points where needed in the groups of sentences below.

1. I ran an ad in the newspaper   At first the results were encouraging

2. It looked like it would be easy to get a job   I got lots of calls

3. I was looking for day work   I said in the ad I would work part-time or full-time

4. What went wrong   I'm still unemployed   Why do you think that is

5. Wow   This is really a surprise

6. Did my husband help you plan the party   Who else helped   How did you keep it a secret

7. Help   This is an emergency

8. Is she still alive   I heard the ambulance   Did it come right away

9. You were asleep when your mother called   I told her you would be up soon   She asked if you were feeling better

10. How many planets are in the solar system

11. Is the moon considered a planet

12. There are nine planets in the solar system   Moons are not planets

13. What is a cutlass

14. A cutlass is a kind of sword   It can also be a kind of fish

15. Do you know the difference between a cutlass fish, a cuttle-fish, and a cusk

2. COMMAS

Commas tell the reader when to pause while reading a sentence. Commas are used in lists, to **set** something **off**, and to add information.

When you see a lot of commas in a sentence, it may be because part of the sentence includes a list. This can be a list of people, actions, places, or anything else.

Marla, Bill, Ed, Barbara, and I went to the game.
Walter plans to paint the house, trim the trees, fix the roof, and clean the gutters.

Sometimes items in a list are connected with the word *or*.

We could use the time to eat lunch, go shopping, or see a movie.

When you write a list as part of a sentence, put a comma after each thing on the list. You can leave out the comma before the words *and* and *or* if you want to. The words *and* and *or* divide the last two things on the list anyway. Never put a comma AFTER the word *and* or *or* in this kind of sentence.

Commas can change the meaning of a sentence. Look at the different **versions** of the same sentence below.

1) They serve pizza, roast, beef sandwiches, and salads.
2) They serve pizza, roast beef, sandwiches, and salads.
3) They serve pizza, roast beef sandwiches, and salads.

Suppose the restaurant serves only three things. Which sentence is correct? The last sentence (3) is the only one that lists three items.

Supply the missing commas in the sentence at the top of the following page.

The seven continents are Asia Africa North America South America Europe Australia and Antarctica.

In this sentence, you need to put commas after *Asia, Africa, North America, South America,* and *Europe.* You can also put a comma after *Australia.* Remember that the comma before *and* is **optional.**

OPTIONAL. Not necessary.

As you add more **details** to your writing, you use more commas. You use commas to set off words and phrases that describe nouns in your sentences. These descriptive phrases often start with the words *who* and *which.* Here are some examples:

DETAIL. A fact or piece of information.

My brother, who is not rich, can't afford to come this year.
Her dog, a collie, is like a member of the family.
The corner house, which is for sale, belongs to my aunt.

Take away the information between the commas, and you still have complete sentences.

My brother can't afford to come this year.
Her dog is like a member of the family.
The corner house belongs to my aunt.

The commas are used on both sides of the phrase to show the reader that you are interrupting the sentence to give more information about the subject of the sentence.

Information that is set off is not always found in the middle of a sentence. In the following examples, this information is at the end of the sentences.

Last year we visited my cousin, who is a student at the University of Texas.
We ate at Le Bistro, a rather expensive restaurant.

Names, short exclamations, and words like *yes* and *no* are often set off from the rest of a sentence. This happens when such words come at the beginning, middle, or end of the sentence. For example:

Hey, how are you?

Yes, I hope to see you again, Tom.

I told you, Jessie, we'll always be friends.

In the last sentence, notice that there are commas on both sides of the word *Jessie*. This is because it appears in the middle of the sentence.

*F*OR YOUR INFORMATION

The Semicolon

The semicolon (;) shows a stronger separation than a comma. But it isn't as strong as a period.

Sometimes you may write two sentences that are very closely related, like these:

We enjoy tennis. We play every day.

He's a Republican. He voted for Reagan.

It would be incorrect to link the two sentences with commas. But you may want to show the reader that the sentences are closely related, so you use a semicolon to connect them.

We enjoy tennis; we play every day.

He's a Republican; he voted for Reagan.

Self-Test

Put an X next to the sentence with the comma used incorrectly.

1. _____ (1) The preamble to the Constitution discusses life, liberty, and the pursuit of happiness.

   _____ (2) The preamble to the Constitution discusses life, liberty and the pursuit of happiness.

   _____ (3) The preamble to the Constitution discusses, life, liberty, and, the pursuit of happiness.

   _____ (4) None of the sentences are correct.

   _____ (5) All of the sentences are correct.

2. _____ (1) His boss, Ms. Hayden is pleased with his work.

   _____ (2) Vince Lombardi was the coach of the Green Bay Packers, a football team from Wisconsin.

   _____ (3) Mark Spitz, a swimmer, won six gold medals.

   _____ (4) She once met Jackie Robinson, a famous baseball player.

   _____ (5) All of the sentences are correct.

3. _____ (1) How are you, Dr. Garcia?

   _____ (2) Gee, I didn't know that.

   _____ (3) Yes, I think so.

   _____ (4) Oh, I guess so.

   _____ (5) All of the sentences are correct.

4. _____ (1) Now, Max, you don't really mean that.

   _____ (2) Look, Sally, I have to leave now.

   _____ (3) No, I can't help you.

   _____ (4) Yes, Rene, I, would like more cake.

   _____ (5) All of the sentences are correct.

Put an X next to the sentence with incorrect punctuation.

5. _____ (1) We ate there last night, the food was excellent.

   _____ (2) We ate there last night; the food was excellent.

   _____ (3) We ate there last night. The food was excellent.

   _____ (4) All of the sentences are incorrect.

   _____ (5) All of the sentences are correct.

6. _____ (1) The sky is growing dark. It's going to rain.

   _____ (2) The sky is growing dark; it's going to rain.

   _____ (3) The sky is growing dark, it's going to rain.

   _____ (4) All of the sentences are incorrect.

   _____ (5) All of the sentences are correct.

3. APOSTROPHES AND QUOTATION MARKS

A very convenient form of punctuation is the apostrophe ('). The apostrophe is used when you write about possession or when you use **contractions** in your writing.

CONTRACTION. Two words joined together to form one word.

An apostrophe is used to show possession in the following sentences:

We watched the game on Harry's TV.
Ellen borrowed Mary's sweater.

Both these sentences show correct use of the apostrophe. The apostrophes tell the reader that the TV belongs to Harry and the sweater belongs to Mary.

Contractions—words like *can't, I'm, we'll, I'd,* and *doesn't*— are used often in conversation and writing. These words are used instead of *cannot, I am, we will, I would,* and *does not.* In all contractions, the apostrophe takes the place of a missing letter or letters. Look at the following paragraph from a campaign speech.

It is time that the people of this state look critically at each candidate. I am the only one who is truly qualified to be your governor. If elected, I will lower taxes, end unemployment, and encourage industry to build their factories in our state. My opponent cannot make these claims. You are informed voters; you will make the difference in this election.

Rewrite the paragraph with as many contractions as possible.

_____

_____

_____

_____

_____

Your rewritten version should have these contractions: It's, I'm, who's, I'll, can't, You're, you'll.

When you write and want to show exactly what someone said, you use quotation marks. Quotation marks tell the reader that you are giving someone's exact words.

"Where are you going?" asked the cab driver.
"I will never raise taxes," promised the candidate.

A **quotation** usually begins with a capital letter. There is always some kind of punctuation mark at the end of the quotation. It comes before the quotation mark.

QUOTATION. Someone's exact words.

When you write a question in quotation marks, always put a question mark before the last set of quotation marks.

"Why do you want to know?" she asked.
She asked, "Why do you want to know?"

If you are quoting a statement, put a period or a comma before the last set of quotation marks.

"This is important," he said.
He said, "This is important."

When you write about people's statements without using their exact words, you do not use quotation marks.

The cab driver asked where we were going.
The candidate promised not to raise taxes.

Look at the following sentence:
The student says the teacher is ignorant.

This sentence could have two different meanings and could be written in two other ways. Different punctuation changes the meaning as to who is ignorant. Now look at these sentences.

The student says, "The teacher is ignorant."
"The student," says the teacher, "is ignorant."

 **Self-Test**

Answer the questions. Then compare your answers with those in *Answers and Explanations* on page 43.

Add periods, question marks, exclamation points, commas, apostrophes, and quotation marks to the sentences.

1. You have the right to remain silent, began the police officer.

2. The defendant, Malcolm Miller continued to proclaim his innocence.

3. I didn't do it he shouted.

4. Sir, said the judge, don't you think I've heard these claims before

5. You have the best lawyer money can buy, said Buddy.

6. My wife, our son, our two daughters my mother and I are spending Christmas together.

7. "Yes you could all come to my house next year suggested my mother.

8. "Say, that's a great idea exclaimed our son.

By adding quotation marks and commas, write two versions of the sentence below.

9. The boss said Natalie was incompetent.

   a. _____

   b. _____

Some of these sentences need apostrophes. Write apostrophes where they are needed.

10. An explorers life is full of adventures and surprises.

11. Christopher Columbus and his men found America while searching for the shores of India.

12. Cartier explored Canadas coast.

13. Ponce de Leons adventures included searching for a fountain of youth.

14. Magellan crossed the worlds oceans.

THINKING AND WRITING

1. Write a sentence listing four or more things you need to buy the next time you go shopping.

_____

_____

_____

2. Write two questions someone might ask you at a job interview.

a. _____

_____

b. _____

_____

3. Think about the conversations you have had recently. Write two sentences that someone said to you. Give the person's name and quote his or her exact words.

a. _____

_____

b. _____

_____

4. Think about the job you have, or a job you'd like to have. Write two or three sentences and tell why you are qualified for the job.

_____

_____

_____

_____

Compare your answers with those in *Answers and Explanations* on page 44.

STRATEGIES FOR SUCCESS

KNOWING WHERE TO PUNCTUATE

Every sentence ends with a punctuation mark. Many sentences have punctuation within them too.

STRATEGY 1: Train your ears to hear the changes.

Talk out what you're writing. Try to hear the pauses and the stops.

Example: Here is part of a cereal ad. First read it aloud. Then add the punctuation you think is missing.

Hey kids
Are you tired of eating the same cereal every morning
Do you wish you could have a change
But does Mom say no to all those sugary cereals
Then try Corn Stars

Three sentences probably sound alike as you read them aloud—the three questions beginning with *Are*, *Do*, and *But does*. They should end with question marks. *Hey kids* is a greeting to get attention. It should have a comma after *Hey* and an exclamation point at the end. The last sentence should end with a period.

Write: Read the rest of the ad on the next page.
1. Add punctuation at the end of each sentence. Add commas where you hear pauses in the middle of the sentences.
2. In the blank at the end of the ad, write your own sentence to end the ad.

It's a delicious new breakfast cereal It has no sugar or preservatives But it's packed with vitamins minerals and real corn You'll love it And so will Mom

---

STRATEGY 2: Always reread what you write.

Be sure every sentence ends with the correct punctuation mark. Be sure commas separate ideas or things in a list.

Example: Look at the title and the paragraph. Which two sentences need different punctuation at the end? Which sentence needs two commas?

> *When was the first dinosaur fossil discovered.*
>
> Some strange large old teeth were found in England in 1822. Everyone wondered what kind of teeth they were?

The title is a question; it should end with a question mark. The first sentence needs commas after *strange* and *large*. The last sentence is a statement; it should end with a period.

Write: Each sentence in the paragraph below has a punctuation error. Correct the sentences.

> *Who discovered the first dinosaur teeth.*
>
> Mary Ann Mantell the wife of Dr. Gideon Mantell discovered the first fossil teeth. The Mantells sent the fossils to the French scientist Baron Cuvier. They hoped he would know what kind of teeth they were?

_____

_____

_____

_____

_____

Compare your answers with those in *Answers and Explanations* on page 44.

Answers and Explanations

1. SENTENCE ENDINGS

1. I ran an ad in the newspaper. At first the results were encouraging.
2. It looked like it would be easy to get a job. I got lots of calls.
3. I was looking for day work. I said in the ad I would work part-time or full-time.
4. What went wrong? I'm still unemployed. Why do you think that is?
5. Wow! This is really a surprise!
6. Did my husband help you plan the party? Who else helped? How did you keep it a secret?
7. Help! This is an emergency!
8. Is she still alive? I heard the ambulance. Did it come right away?
9. You were asleep when your mother called. I told her you would be up soon. She asked if you were feeling better.
10. How many planets are in the solar system?
11. Is the moon considered a planet?
12. There are nine planets in the solar system. Moons are not planets.
13. What is a cutlass?
14. A cutlass is a kind of sword. It can also be a kind of fish.
15. Do you know the difference between a cutlass fish, a cuttlefish, and a cusk?

2. COMMAS

1. (3) There should be no commas after *discusses* and *and*.
2. (1) There should be commas on both sides of *Ms. Hayden*.
3. (5) The commas are used correctly in all the sentences.
4. (4) There should be no commas between *I* and *would*.
5. (1) Two complete sentences shouldn't be joined by a comma.
6. (3) Two complete sentences shouldn't be joined by a comma.

3. THE APOSTROPHE AND QUOTATION MARKS

1. "You have the right to remain silent," began the police officer.

   Exact quotes are enclosed in quotation marks.

2. The defendant, Malcolm Miller, continued to proclaim his innocence.

   A comma is added after *Miller* so that the name is correctly set off from the rest of the sentence.

3. "I didn't do it!" he shouted.

   Quotation marks surround the exact words. Since the words were shouted, an exclamation point is used. An apostrophe is added to the contraction *didn't*.

4. "Sir," said the judge, "don't you think I've heard these claims before?"

   Quotation marks surround the judge's exact words. The judge's words are a question, so they're followed by a question mark. *Don't* and *I've* are contractions and need apostrophes.

5. "You have the best lawyer money can buy," said Buddy.

   Quotation marks surround the sentence, which is an exact quote.

6. My wife, your son, our two daughters, my mother, and I are spending Christmas together.

   A comma is added to separate *daughters* and *my mother*. Another comma can be added after *mother*, but the sentence is correct without it.

7. "Yes, you could all come to my house next year," suggested my mother.

   A comma is added to separate *yes* from the rest of the sentence. A comma and quotation marks are added after *year* to show where the mother's exact words end.

8. "Say, that's a great idea!" exclaimed our son.

   An exclamation point and quotation marks show the end of the son's words.

9. a. "The boss," said Natalie, "was incompetent."

   b. The boss said, "Natalie was incompetent."

10. An explorer's life is full of adventures and surprises. (An explorer's life's full of adventures and surprises.)

11. No apostrophes are needed in this sentence.
12. Cartier explored <u>Canada's</u> coast.
13. Ponce de <u>Leon's</u> adventures included searching for a fountain of youth.
14. Magellan crossed the <u>world's</u> oceans.

THINKING AND WRITING

There are many ways to answer the questions. Here are some examples.

1. I need milk, bread, peanut butter, and ice cream.
2. a. Why do you want this job?
   b. Why did you leave your last job?
3. a. Pat asked, "Can you come over for dinner?"
   b. Alan said, "This has been a rotten day."
4.   I'd like a job as a paramedic. I think I'm qualified for this kind of work because I know a lot about first aid. Also, I'm very patient, and I like to help people.

STRATEGIES FOR SUCCESS

Strategy 1

It's a delicious new breakfast cereal<u>.</u> It has no sugar or preservatives<u>.</u> But it's packed with vitamins<u>,</u> minerals<u>,</u> and real corn<u>.</u> You'll love it<u>.</u> And so will Mom<u>.</u>
<u>Get some today.</u>

Strategy 2

Who discovered the first dinosaur teeth<u>?</u>

Mary Ann Mantell<u>,</u> the wife of Dr. Gideon Mantell<u>,</u> discovered the first fossil teeth. The Mantells sent the fossils to the French scientist<u>,</u> Baron Cuvier. They hoped he would know what kind of teeth they were<u>.</u>

WRITING CLEAR SENTENCES

BOOKS, magazine articles, and letters from home are made of sentences. Grocery lists and clothing tags are not. Recipes, warranties, and step-by-step instructions are made of sentences. Most movie titles and want-ad headlines are not.

Why bother to use sentences? Isn't any kind of communication all right as long as it is understood? Do you know a sentence when you see it? How can you be sure?

These questions are answered in this unit. In this unit, you will begin to explore the process of writing clear sentences.

1. SENTENCES THAT MAKE SENSE

When you fill out a job application, you may be asked to write why you think you are qualified for the job. When you sign your child's report card, you might want to include a note to the teacher. When your neighbor dies, you might wish to write a note to his family. When you get poor service, you might want to write a letter of complaint.

In all of these situations, you can best get your message across if you use **complete sentences.** Look at two examples:

Why do you think you are qualified for this job?

HARD WORKER

NEED WORK BAD

Why do you think you are qualified for this job?

I work hard and fast. I did metal work in Texas before moving here. In three years I was never out sick.

Which person would you hire? The first person doesn't seem very interested in the job. The person uses **incomplete sentences** and doesn't give you much information. The second person takes the time to write good, complete sentences. He or she makes a good impression.

Look at Henry and Sheila. Who is talking in sentences? If you're not sure, try this test. First, read only Henry's words. Then read only Sheila's. Which person is communicating complete thoughts?

People often talk in incomplete sentences. And they may understand one another very well. But writing is different. You should almost always use complete sentences when you write.

Henry used three complete sentences. Sheila used none. Looking just at Sheila's words, we have the following:

1. Cooking vegetables for dinner
2. And watching TV
3. In a couple of hours
4. Betty

These aren't sentences because information is missing from each group of words.

WHO is cooking vegetables?
WHO was watching TV?
WHAT will happen in a couple of hours?
WHAT will Betty do?

Keep these questions in mind. Now rewrite Sheila's four statements, changing them into four sentences.

HENRY   **SHEILA**

1. _____

_____

2. _____

_____

3. _____

_____

4. _____

_____

To be complete, a sentence must have two things: a **subject** and a **predicate.** The subject identifies the main WHO or WHAT in the sentence. The subject usually includes a noun (Betty, woman) or pronoun (she). The predicate tells what the subject IS or DOES. It always includes a **verb.**

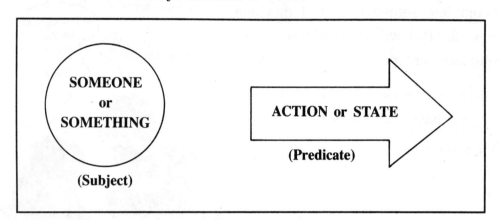

SOMEONE or SOMETHING

(Subject)

ACTION or STATE

(Predicate)

Sheila's first two sentences on page 47 have incomplete predicates (part of the verb is missing) and no subjects. We often talk this way. But in writing, we should use complete sentences. For example, we would write:

<u>I was</u> cooking dinner.
<u>We were</u> watching TV.

Sheila's last answer needs a predicate. We need to know who Betty is or what she does. We could write:

Betty <u>will drive me to my class</u>.

Sheila's third sentence needs both a subject and a predicate. If <u>my class</u> is the subject and <u>start</u> is what the class does, we might write:

My class starts in a couple of hours.

Complete sentences don't have to be long. They don't need a lot of words. For example, these are sentences:

1. My boss quit.
2. She did.
3. It was.
4. The kids went.
5. The old man won.

The last word in each of these sentences is the predicate. It is also the verb. The other words make up the subject.

In longer sentences, it is still easy to identify the subjects and predicates. Look at these sentences. The subjects are circled. The predicates are underlined.

1. (My boss) quit his job after seven years.
2. (She) did it again.

Circle the subjects and underline the predicates in the sentences below.

3. It was fun to be alone.
4. The kids went home after the game.
5. The old man won the lottery.

The part of the sentences that includes the verbs (was, went, won) should be underlined. Those words make up the predicates. The other words, the words in front of the verb, should be circled. They make up the subjects.

FOR YOUR INFORMATION

Stop!   Wait!
                                        Forget it!
            Read this!
    Look!
                        Don't worry!

These are sentences too. They are commands. They are telling the reader (you) to do something. The subject of each of these sentences is *you*.

Self-Test

Circle the subject and underline the predicate in these sentences.

1. She writes to her parents every week.
2. Her parents wait to get those letters.
3. Her letters are important to them.
4. Most of the time, she just writes about her job.
5. Sometimes she tells them about her friends.
6. They wonder if she misses them.

7. Now find the verbs in the sentences above. Write them in the blanks.

   a. _____   b. _____   c. _____

   d. _____   e. _____   f. _____

The following groups of words are not sentences. Rewrite the statements, adding words to make complete sentences.

8. works very hard because she has two jobs

   _____

   _____

9. the newspaper I read most often

   _____

   _____

10. the greatest athletes this country has ever known

    _____

    _____

11. after getting out of prison

    _____

    _____

12. celebrated all weekend

    _____

    _____

2. REACHING AGREEMENT

Subject-verb agreement is an important part of good writing. Subject-verb agreement means using the correct verb form with the subject of the sentence. Look at these sentences.

The <u>girls</u> <u>eat</u> lunch together every day.
One <u>girl</u> <u>eats</u> alone.

Notice that girl<u>s</u> eat and girl eat<u>s</u>. When the subject is **plural** (ends in *s*), the verb has no *s*. When the subject is **singular,** the verb ends in *s*.

Complete these sentences with the correct word in parentheses. Write the word in the blank.

1. The President _____ each bill into law. (sign/signs)
2. My parents _____ to church every Sunday. (go/goes)
3. Children today _____ too much TV. (watch/watches)

The answers are: signs, go, watch. The word *children* is plural even though it doesn't end in *s*.

Subject-verb agreement can be tricky with the **present tense** of the verbs *be* and *have*. Look at the charts below.

PRESENT TENSE OF THE VERBS *BE* AND *HAVE*

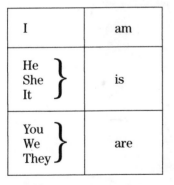

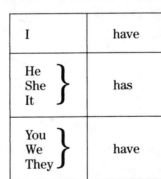

I	am
He She It	is
You We They	are

I	have
He She It	has
You We They	have

Complete the sentences on the next page. Use the correct form of *be* in the first sentence. Use the correct form of *have* in the second sentence.

She _____ the first-place winner.

He _____ a prize for you.

You should never write *I be, you be, he be, we be,* or *they be.* And you shouldn't write *you is.*

The verb *have* is easy in the **past tense.** It's always *had.* But the verb *be* can be tricky in the past tense too. You should never write *you was, we was,* or *they was.* Look at this chart.

PAST TENSE OF *BE*

I	was
He She It }	was
You We They }	were

PAST TENSE. The forms of a verb that express past time— what someone or something was like or what happened before.

---

*F*OR YOUR INFORMATION

Work. Watch. Worry. These are three verbs with three different ways of forming the third-person singular verb form—the verb form that you use with *he, she,* and *it.* With all verbs except *be* and *have* and special words like *can, must, will, may, might,* and *should,* you add the letters *s, es,* or *ies* to the verb.

Add *-s* to most verbs.	Add *-es* to verbs ending in *ch* (watch), *sh* (wash), or *s* (pass).	Change the *y* to *i* and add *-es* to verbs ending in *y.**
WORK	WATCH	WORRY
I work	I watch	I worry
He She It } work<u>s</u>	He She It } watch<u>es</u>	He She It } worr<u>ies</u>
You We They } work	You We They } watch	You We They } worry

*Watch out for the exception: He bu<u>ys</u>.

Self-Test

Answer the questions. Then compare your answers with those in *Answers and Explanations* on page 63.

Complete the sentences with the correct word in parentheses. Write the word in the blank.

1. Although he is retired, he still _____ ten laps a day. (swim/swims)

2. On the whole, women _____ healthier than men. (be/is/are)

3. The ceremony _____ in ten minutes. (start/starts)

4. She _____ six children. (have/has)

5. We _____ going to tell you. (was/were)

6. She _____ the same work that her mother _____. (do/does)

Put an X next to the word or words that are NOT a correct and complete sentence.

7. ___ (1) Is.
   ___ (2) Stop.
   ___ (3) Look.
   ___ (4) Listen.
   ___ (5) Leave.

8. ___ (1) Employment opportunities here are good.
   ___ (2) Opportunities are good.
   ___ (3) Opportunities are here.
   ___ (4) Opportunities is here.
   ___ (5) Opportunity is here.

9. ___ (1) The average human stomach hold at least a quart of food.
   ___ (2) The average human stomach holds at least a quart of food.
   ___ (3) Most human stomachs hold at least a quart of food.
   ___ (4) Most human stomachs can hold at least a quart of food.
   ___ (5) The average human stomach can hold at least a quart of food.

10. ___ (1) A triangle is a three-sided polygon.
    ___ (2) A triangle is a flat three-sided drawing.
    ___ (3) An equilateral triangle has three equal sides.
    ___ (4) An obtuse triangle has one side that is longer than the other two.
    ___ (5) An isosceles triangle be shaped like a Christmas tree.

3. RUN-ON SENTENCES AND FRAGMENTS

Run-on sentences seem to have been written by someone who doesn't know when to stop. The words run on and on. The writer may have one or more complete sentences linked together. Separate ideas need to be separated into separate sentences. Look at the following examples:

1. I can't believe I ate the whole thing it was delicious.
2. The bill was very popular among the farmers back home the senator said he would vote for it.
3. The basketball team ended its three-game losing streak tonight they won 87–86.

Were the above sentences clear and easy to understand? Did you have to reread any of them because the meaning was unclear the first time? Look back at the sentences and draw a slash mark (/) where you think a sentence should end.

Each of the three examples above has two complete ideas. Each example consists of two **independent clauses**. Each example can be divided into two sentences, like this:

1. I can't believe I ate the whole thing! It was delicious!
2. The bill was very popular among the farmers back home. The senator said he would vote for it.

Or you can keep the words in a single sentence, separating the independent clauses, like this:

3. The basketball team ended its three-game losing streak tonight; they won 87–86.

To write well, you need to know a sentence from a **sentence fragment.** This is not always easy to do. Some sentence fragments are very long. They look like sentences. And they are often mistakenly used in place of sentences.

For example, phrases that answer the questions *when?* or *why?* often begin with such words as *while, before, after,* and *because.* These phrases are not sentences. They are sentence fragments. Here are two fragments:

Because I couldn't stand her nagging.
While she was working days at the hospital.

And here are two sentences:

I left.
Mary went to school at night.

In these examples, the fragments are longer than the sentences. But the sentences sound more complete. There are two ways to make a fragment into a sentence.

1. Add the fragment to a complete sentence (an independent clause).
2. Cut off the first word of the fragment.

Your choice would depend on how much information you want to give the reader.

Let's try the first way. After combining the fragments with the sentences, you have the following:

Because I couldn't stand her nagging, I left.
While she was working days at the hospital, Mary went to school at night.

You could also say this:

I left because I couldn't stand her nagging.
Mary went to school at night while she was working days at the hospital.

You can combine fragments and sentences in either order. It just depends on what sounds right to you. In all these versions, the subjects and predicates are the same as they were in the short sentences above (I left, Mary went to school at night).

The second way to turn fragments into sentences is to cut off the first word. These are complete sentences:

I couldn't stand her nagging.

She was working days at the hospital.

This method will not turn all fragments into sentences. You can test whether you have a sentence by looking for the subjects and predicates. *I* and *She* are the subjects. The remaining words of each sentence are the predicates.

Another kind of fragment begins with a word ending in *-ing*. These fragments need to be fixed differently. Usually a subject and part of the predicate need to be added to make this kind of fragment into a sentence. See if you can fix these fragments by making them into sentences.

1. Answering questions at the press conference
2. Telling her to leave

1. _____
   _____
2. _____
   _____

You might have simply added a subject and verb, creating sentences such as these:

1. The president was answering questions at the press conference.
2. He kept telling her to leave.

Or, you might have lengthened the sentences even more, ending up with one like this:

Before telling her to leave, he asked for his ring back.

Self-Test

Answer the questions. Then compare your answers with those in *Answers and Explanations* on page 63.

Write an S in the blank next to each sentence.
Write an F in the blank next to each fragment.

1. _____ While doing my grocery shopping on Saturday.

2. _____ I saw her.

3. _____ Before I could say a word.

4. _____ She came up to me and started talking about my sister.

5. _____ Going on and on about my sister and some people that I've never even met before.

6. _____ She seems nice enough.

7. _____ A little on the talkative side maybe.

8. _____ But nice.

Put an X next to the group of words that is a correct sentence or that are sentences.

9. _____ (1) Because he didn't have time.

_____ (2) Because he didn't have time for breakfast.

_____ (3) He didn't have time for breakfast.

_____ (4) A huge lunch, because he didn't have time for breakfast.

_____ (5) A huge lunch of meatballs and spaghetti, because he didn't have time for breakfast.

10. _____ (1) The agency has a contract to buy the building it has already bought others in the neighborhood.

_____ (2) They have a contract to buy the building they have already bought others in the neighborhood.

_____ (3) The agency has a contract to buy the building, it has already.

_____ (4) The agency has a contract to buy the building, it has already bought others in the neighborhood.

_____ (5) The agency has a contract to buy the building. It has already bought others in the neighborhood.

11. _____ (1) My parents were divorced five years ago, I stayed with my mother.

_____ (2) My parents were divorced five years ago. I stayed with my mother.

_____ (3) My parents were divorced five years ago I stayed with my mother.

_____ (4) My parents were divorced. Five years ago. I stayed with my mother.

_____ (5) My parents were divorced five years. Ago I stayed with my mother.

Put an X next to the best way to change each group of words into a complete sentence. Then write the corrected sentence in the space.

12. After I told him goodbye.
_____ (1) Add the words and good luck.
_____ (2) Take away the word him.
_____ (3) Take away the word After.
_____ (4) Take away the word goodbye.
_____ (5) No change is needed.

_____
_____

13. You still has the television on.
_____ (1) Add the words the table.
_____ (2) Add the words too loud.
_____ (3) Take away the word You.
_____ (4) Change the word has to have.
_____ (5) No change is needed.

_____
_____

14. Because the foreman yelled at her.
_____ (1) Add the words She left.
_____ (2) Add the word loudly.
_____ (3) Take away the words at her.
_____ (4) Take away the words the foreman.
_____ (5) No change is needed.

_____
_____

15. The rooms is clean.
_____ (1) Add the word after.
_____ (2) Add the word Because.
_____ (3) Change the word is to be.
_____ (4) Change the word is to are.
_____ (5) No change is needed.

_____
_____

16. Always saying he's going to quit smoking.
_____ (1) Add the word he.
_____ (2) Add the words He is.
_____ (3) Take away the word going.
_____ (4) Take away the word smoking.
_____ (5) No change is needed.

_____
_____

THINKING AND WRITING

1. Think about something you did at home yesterday or today. Write three complete sentences about what you did.

_____

_____

_____

_____

2. Think about something that you want to remind a friend or family member to do. Write it as a sentence.

_____

_____

3. Think about something you own that is important to you. This could be a car, family Bible, or a piece of furniture that has been in the family for a long time. It could be a piece of jewelry or anything else that you value. Write two or more sentences to describe it.

_____

_____

_____

_____

Compare your answers with those in *Answers and Explanations* on page 64.

STRATEGIES FOR SUCCESS

1. WRITING CLEAR SENTENCES

To be clear, a sentence must have a definite subject and predicate.

STRATEGY: Plan what you write.

Plan the subject and the predicate: WHO or WHAT is doing something? And what are they DOING?

Example: Imagine that you are writing a letter to your relatives. You want to tell them about your husband's or wife's new job, and about your child's new school. What would the subjects and predicates of the sentences be?

	Subjects		Predicates
1.	husband (Ed)	a.	has a new job
		b.	works at the radio station
2.	son (Dave)	a.	loves his new school
		b.	is on the baseball team

Once you've planned the ideas, the letter might look like this:

> Ed and Dave are fine. Ed has a new job. He works at the radio station now. Dave loves his new school. He's on the baseball team.

Write: Imagine that a friend is trying to find an apartment and has given your name as a reference. Plan the ideas you might include in a letter of reference for your friend.

	Subject		Predicates
1.	_____	a.	_____
		b.	_____

Complete the reference letter with the subject and predicates you planned on page 60.

I have know _____ for more than _____ years. _____

_____

_____

_____. She would be a good tenant.

2. CORRECTING NON-SENTENCES

Run-on sentences and fragments make your writing confusing to read.

STRATEGY: Always reread what you write.

If you find run-on sentences or groups of words that aren't complete sentences, rewrite them.

Example: Which groups of words in this note aren't sentences?

Went to the plant yesterday. Because I want to go back to work. Closed again. Don't know why. Don't know what to do or who to call. Maybe Pete.

None of the groups of words are sentences. None of them have subjects. The last group is missing a predicate too.

Write: Rewrite the note above. Change all the fragments into sentences. The first one is done for you.

I went to the plant yesterday because I want to go back to work. _____

_____

_____

_____

Compare your answers with those in *Answers and Explanations* on page 64.

Answers and Explanations

1. SENTENCES THAT MAKE SENSE

1. (She) writes to her parents every week.

    She is the person who performs the action (writes to her parents every week). Everything after *She* is the predicate.

2. (Her parents) wait to get those letters.

    This time, *her parents* do something (wait to get those letters).

3. (Her letters) are important to them.

    Here, *her letters* is the subject of the sentence.

4. Most of the time, (she) just writes about her job.

    She does something (just writes about her job).

5. Sometimes (she) tells them about her friends.

    She is the subject. The rest of the sentence is the predicate.

6. (They) wonder if she misses them.

    They (parents) do something (wonder if she misses them).

7. a. writes   b. wait   c. are   d. writes   e. tells   f. wonder

You can write the sentences in many ways. Here are some sample answers.

8. She works very hard because she has two jobs.

    This is a complete sentence now that it has a subject (She).

9. The *Post* is the newspaper I read most often.

    The newspaper I read most often is the *Post*.

    Either version is correct. *The Post* is the subject of the first sentence; *The newspaper* is the subject of the second. In both versions, a verb (*is*) was added.

10. Hank Aaron is one of the greatest athletes this country has ever known.

    They are the greatest athletes this country has ever known.

    You need to add a subject (*Hank Aaron* or *They*) and a verb (*is* or *are*).

11. After getting out of prison, he tried to find a job.

    He tried to find a job after getting out of prison.

    A subject and verb are needed to make it a sentence. (*He* is the subject; *tried* is the verb.)

12. The team celebrated all weekend.

   This is a complete sentence now that it has a subject (*The team*).

2. REACHING AGREEMENT

1. Although he is retired, he still <u>swims</u> ten laps a day.

2. On the whole, women <u>are</u> healthier than men.

3. The ceremony <u>starts</u> in ten minutes.

4. She <u>has</u> six children.

5. We <u>were</u> going to tell you.

6. She <u>does</u> the same work that her mother <u>does</u>.

7. (1) is the answer. All the others are commands, making them complete sentences with *You* as the subject.

8. (4) is the answer. The subject and verb do not agree. They do agree in answers (3) and (5).

9. (1) is the answer. The subject and verb do not agree. You have to write <u>stomach *holds*</u> or <u>stomachs *hold*</u>.

10. (5) is the answer. It isn't correct to write <u>A triangle be</u>. You have to write <u>A triangle is</u>.

3. RUN-ON SENTENCES AND FRAGMENTS

1. <u>F</u> While doing my grocery shopping on Saturday.
   This is a fragment telling *when*.

2. <u>S</u> I saw her.
   This is a complete sentence, with *I* as the subject and *saw* as the verb.

3. <u>F</u> Before I could say a word.
   This is another fragment that answers the question *when*.

4. <u>S</u> She came up to me and started talking about my sister.
   In this sentence, *she* is the subject. There are two verbs, *came* and *started talking*.

5. <u>F</u> Going on and on about my sister and some people that I've never even met before.
   This group of words is missing a subject. WHO was going on and on?

6. <u>S</u> She seems nice enough.
   She is the subject; *seems* is the verb.

7. <u>F</u> A little on the talkative side maybe.
   Both subject and verb are missing.

8. <u>F</u> But nice.
   Both subject and verb are missing again.

9. (3) is the correct answer. (1), (2), (4), and (5) are fragments.

10. (5) is the correct answer. (1), (2), and (3) are run-on sentences. (4) is a run-on sentence too, because two independent clauses are connected by a comma.

11. (2) is the correct answer. (1) and (3) are run-on sentences. (4) and (5) contain fragments.

12. (3) is the correct answer: <u>I told him goodbye.</u>

13. (4) is the correct answer: <u>You still have the television on.</u>

14. (1) is the correct answer: <u>She left because the foreman yelled at her./Because the foreman yelled at her, she left.</u>

15. (4) is the correct answer: <u>The rooms are clean.</u>

16. (2) is the correct answer: <u>He is always saying he's going to quit smoking.</u>

THINKING AND WRITING

You can answer the questions in many ways. Here are some sample answers.

1. I cleaned the kitchen. I got the children ready for school. I made a chicken stew.

2. Please pick up your clothes and take out the trash.

3. A quilt my grandmother made is valuable to me. I hope to give it to my daughter someday when she has a family. It is old but very beautiful.

STRATEGIES FOR SUCCESS

You can write the answers in many ways. Here are some samples.

1. Writing Clear Sentences

Subject		Predicates	
1. Leslie Watkins	a. has a good job		b. is dependable

I have known Leslie Watkins for more than three years. She has a good job. She is a dependable person. She would be a good tenant.

2. Correcting Non-Sentences.

I went to the plant yesterday because I want to go back to work. It was closed again. I don't know why. I don't know what to do or who to call. Maybe I'll try Pete.

NOUNS, PRONOUNS, AND ADJECTIVES

THE subjects and objects of sentences usually include nouns or pronouns. Nouns are name words. They identify persons, places, things, animals, or ideas. Pronouns take the place of nouns. Using pronouns often makes sentences easier to read.

Adjectives describe nouns and pronouns. Adjectives help the reader picture the nouns more clearly by describing *which, how many, what color,* or *what kind.*

1. FINDING SUBJECTS AND OBJECTS

You know that every sentence needs a subject and that a subject usually includes a noun or pronoun. But not all nouns or pronouns are subjects. Look at the following incomplete sentences:

Anita wrote _____.
Wilbur ate _____.
The cow jumped over _____.

You might complete these sentences with words like *the letter, the sandwich,* and *the moon.* They are the **objects** of the sentences. An object answers the question *who?* or *what?* after the verb in a sentence.

Do the above groups of words need objects in order to be complete sentences? No. They are all sentences:

Anita wrote.   Wilbur ate.   The cow jumped over.

But we can't always write simple, short sentences. When the ideas need to be more complete, we have to add objects to our sentences. Objects give the reader a clearer picture of what is happening. Here's a diagram of a sentence:

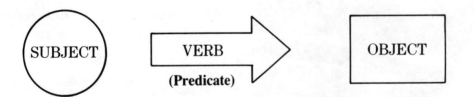

Some people remember the object of the sentence as the thing that has something done to it. The subjects of the sentences on the next page are <u>Doris</u>, <u>Everyone</u>, and <u>Bob</u>. Circle the objects.

Doris read the memo aloud.

Everyone attended the meeting.

Bob married Maria last Saturday.

You are right if you identified the following objects of the sentences: the memo, the meeting, and Maria.

Now write three sentences. Use each of the above nouns as the SUBJECT of a sentence.

1. _____

_____

2. _____

_____

3. _____

_____

Nouns can be subjects or objects in a sentence. It all depends on what you want to emphasize. Writing sentences with THINGS as the subjects may be harder than writing sentences with PEOPLE as the subjects. Here are some ways you might write sentences using the words above as subjects:

The memo was four pages long.

The meeting lasted longer than we expected.

Maria wore a beautiful dress.

Nouns that are subjects of sentences are usually names of persons, places, things, or animals. Nouns can also be ideas or even verb forms. Here are some examples. The subjects of the sentences are underlined.

Exercise is as important as diet.

Religion is an important part of his life.

Life is unfair.

Jogging is good exercise.

The last sentence has a verb form for a subject (jogging). You can change a verb (jog) to a noun (jogging) by adding -ing.

Sometimes a sentence will have two or more subjects or objects. These are called **compound subjects** or **compound objects.** Here are some examples:

Ron and Nancy went to the ball. (compound subject)
They met George and Barbara there. (compound object)
Death and taxes are certain to affect everyone. (compound subject)
Do you remember John, Paul, George, and Ringo from the sixties? (compound object)

Write a sentence with a compound subject like the ones above.

_____

_____

Write a sentence with a compound object like the ones above.

_____

_____

FOR YOUR INFORMATION

You know that nouns are words that identify persons, places, things, animals, or ideas. But there are two kinds of nouns—common nouns and proper nouns. The difference between the two is shown in the lists below. Common nouns give labels. Proper nouns give names.

COMMON NOUNS	PROPER NOUNS
author	Ralph Waldo Emerson
mayor	Henry Cisneros
city	Dallas
dog	Spot
theater	Kennedy Center

Self-Test

Answer the questions. Then compare your answers with those in *Answers and Explanations* on page 82.

Add subjects and objects to the following groups of words to make sentences.

1. The _____ yelled at the _____

2. _____ went to the _____

3. The _____ prescribed a strong _____

4. _____ felt better after taking the _____

5. _____ can't buy _____

Underline the subject in each sentence below.

6. Love is blind.

7. Fred is in love.

8. Kelly thinks Fred is in love with her.

9. The TV station is where they met.

10. It wasn't a very romantic first meeting.

11. But Fred and Kelly like to tell the story to friends.

12. Their friends are still surprised that they got together.

13. List two common nouns from the subjects you underlined in sentences 6–12 above.

    a. _____ b. _____

14. List two proper nouns from the subjects you underlined in sentences 6–12 above.

    a. _____ b. _____

Underline the object of each sentence below.

15. Before breakfast, Albert always reads the newspaper.

16. His wife would rather just stare at her coffee.

17. Mark lost his dog while walking in the park.

18. A stranger found him.

2. FORMING PLURALS

When you write about more than one person, place, thing, animal, or idea, you have to form the plural of a noun. Usually you add the letter *s* to the noun.

girl<u>s</u>   gorilla<u>s</u>   river<u>s</u>

But sometimes you have to add more than the letter *s* to form the plural. Some words already end with an *s* sound and need an *-es* ending. If you try to say *boxs*, *beachs*, or *buss*, you can hear the problem. These words sound just like the singular forms, *box*, *beach*, and *bus*. So, with any word that ends in *s*, *sh*, *ch*, *x*, or *z*, add *-es* to form the plural.

b<u>o</u>x<u>es</u>   beach<u>es</u>   bus<u>es</u>

Some singular nouns that end with the letter *y* need only an *s* to form the plural. If the letter before the *y* is a **vowel** (*a*, *e*, *i*, *o*, or *u*), just add *-s* to the end of the word.

boy<u>s</u>   alley<u>s</u>   donkey<u>s</u>

But most nouns that end with the letter *y* have a **consonant** just before the *y*. If the letter before the *y* is any letter other than *a*, *e*, *i*, *o*, or *u*, it's a consonant. With this kind of word, drop the *y* and add *-ies* to form the plural of the word.

lady   → ladi<u>es</u>
mystery → myster<u>ies</u>
party   → parti<u>es</u>

Forming plurals of words that end in *f* or *fe* can be tricky. The general rule is that you drop the *f* or *fe* and add *-ves*. The rule applies to such words as *life*, *loaf*, and *leaf*.

life → li<u>ves</u>
loaf → loa<u>ves</u>
leaf → lea<u>ves</u>

VOWEL. One of these letters of the alphabet: *a, e, i, o,* or *u.*

CONSONANT. Any letter of the alphabet that isn't a vowel.

Following the same rule, write the plurals of these words.

wife _____

elf _____

wolf _____

There are a few words ending in *f* or *fe* that are **exceptions** to the above rule. When forming plurals of these words, just add the letter *s*. The words are:

roof	giraff
chief	cliff
handkerchief	belief

Of course, not all plurals end with the letter *s*. If you are writing about more than one man, woman, or child, for example, you use the words *men, women,* and *children*. Here are some other exceptions—plurals that do not end in the letter *s*. They are probably familiar to you. Write the plurals of these words.

foot _____

mouse _____

tooth _____

You can remember the words that have plurals that don't end in *s* when you remember this sentence: *The feet and teeth of men, women, and children are larger than those of mice.*

Self-Test

Answer the questions. Then compare your answers with those in _Answers and Explanations_ on page 82.

Put an X next to the word that is an incorrect plural noun.

1. ____ (1) giraffes
   ____ (2) halves
   ____ (3) laughs
   ____ (4) baths
   ____ (5) All the words are correct.

2. ____ (1) monkeys
   ____ (2) donkeys
   ____ (3) cookys
   ____ (4) house keys
   ____ (5) All the words are correct.

3. ____ (1) agencies
   ____ (2) ladies
   ____ (3) gentlemans
   ____ (4) children
   ____ (5) All the words are correct.

4. ____ (1) rooves
   ____ (2) houses
   ____ (3) lives
   ____ (4) mice
   ____ (5) All the words are correct.

Write the plural forms of all the underlined nouns.

The cost-cutting process and activity of the space program
have begun. Satellite, shuttle, and rocket are expensive, and we
do not know when future launch will occur. Company contract-
ing with NASA are still involved in controversy about the last
shuttle trip. More journey may not occur for year.

5. _____

6. _____

7. _____

8. _____

9. _____

10. _____

11. _____

12. _____

13. _____

14. _____

3. CHANGING NOUNS TO PRONOUNS

Pronouns are words that take the place of nouns. Without pronouns, sentences would be long and **repetitious.** Look at the example below, where no pronouns are used.

Pocahontas was an American Indian princess. Pocahontas lived during the seventeenth century. Pocahontas's real name was Matoaka; Pocahontas was the daughter of Powhatan. The legend is that Pocahontas saved the life of Captain John Smith. John Smith was, of course, grateful to Pocahontas for that. Some people thought that Pocahontas and Smith might marry, but Pocahontas married John Rolfe in 1614. Pocahontas died in 1617.

A clearer and shorter version of the same text substitutes pronouns for some of the nouns. The pronouns are underlined.

Pocahontas was an American Indian princess. She lived during the seventeenth century. Her real name was Matoaka; she was the daughter of Powhatan. The legend is that she saved the life of Captain John Smith. He was, of course, grateful to her for that. Some people thought that Pocahontas and Smith might marry, but she married John Rolfe in 1614. She died in 1617.

Pronouns are short and easy to use. They make reading easier than if the writer repeats the same nouns over and over.

There is a complete chart of personal pronouns below. The words in the first column can be subjects of a sentence. The words in the last column can be objects of a sentence. The words in the middle column are **possessive pronouns.** They can be subjects or objects.

Subject Pronouns	Possessive Pronouns	Object Pronouns
I	mine	me
you	yours	you
he, she, it	his, hers, its	him, her, it
we	ours	us
you	yours	you
they	theirs	them

Pronouns can make writing briefer and easier to read. But they can also create problems. When using them, be sure your reader can tell who or what you mean by *it, he,* or whatever pronoun you use. Look at the following examples:

The boss told Jack he couldn't be late again.
I'll hold the nail with my right hand. When I nod my head, hit it!

Are you sure of what is happening in these sentences? Who can't be late again—Jack or the boss? What should be hit—the nail, the hand, or the head?

Change the sentences above so that the meaning is clear. You will have to change several words in each sentence.

1. _____
   _____

2. _____
   _____

You may have **eliminated** the pronouns from the sentences when you rewrote them. Your sentences may look like these:

The boss told Jack not to be late again.
Hit the nail when I nod my head.

In the first version of both sentences, the pronouns created confusion because there were at least two possible *he*s and *it*s in the sentences. One way to eliminate the confusion is to eliminate the pronouns. The pronouns were eliminated in the **revised** sentences above.

But you don't need to get rid of the pronouns. Here are two other ways to revise and clarify the sentences:

The boss warned Jack that he shouldn't be late again.
Here's the nail. When I nod, hit it.

In both versions, the pronouns (*he* and *it*) are back. But there is no longer any doubt as to who *he* is or what *it* is.

ELIMINATE. To get rid of.

REVISE. To make changes or corrections.

Self-Test

Answer the questions. Then compare your answers with those in *Answers and Explanations* on page 83.

Underline the pronoun needed to correctly complete these sentences.

1. You and (I/me) should make plans.
2. (We/Us) girls have to stick together.
3. They want to go out with you and (I/me).
4. We want to go with (they/them).
5. She introduced me to (him/he).
6. She went to the party with (he/him).
7. Mine is ready. (Your/Yours) will be ready soon.
8. (He/Him) told (she/her) to come along with (we/us).

Change the underlined words to pronouns. Write the pronouns in the spaces.

9. Halley's comet was a phenomenon of 1986. <u>Halley's comet</u> was at least nine miles long and two miles wide. _____

10. Scientists were intrigued. <u>Scientists</u> thought they saw dust shooting out of the comet when <u>the comet</u> passed by. _____ _____

11. Astronomers knew that <u>astronomers</u> wouldn't be able to study the comet again. _____

12. <u>The comet</u> won't pass by the earth again until the year 2061. _____

Revise these sentences to clarify the meaning of the underlined pronouns.

13. When Holly visited Susan, <u>she</u> told <u>her</u> <u>she</u> was pregnant.

    _____

    _____

14. He dropped the wooden box on his foot and broke <u>it</u>.

    _____

    _____

15. His dog has fleas, and <u>he</u> is always scratching them.

    _____

    _____

4. USING ADJECTIVES TO CLARIFY WRITING

Adjectives are words that are used to describe nouns and pronouns. They are usually placed before the noun they describe.

The <u>nervous</u> <u>young</u> actress got the part.

But adjectives can also come after the verb. Look at the underlined adjectives in the sentences below.

<u>This</u> book is <u>heavy</u>.
<u>This</u> <u>thick</u> <u>blue</u> <u>telephone</u> book is <u>bulky</u> and <u>heavy</u>.

Without adjectives, most sentences wouldn't be very interesting. Adjectives help the reader **visualize** what the writer is describing. Anyone who tries to sell something through writing will use adjectives very carefully. Look at all the adjectives in the menu below.

ADJECTIVE. A word that describes a noun or pronoun. It tells what color, what kind, how many, etc.

VISUALIZE. To see.

WEEKLY SPECIALS

MONDAY:
Hot grilled hamburger on fluffy fresh bun; crisp hot french fries; tossed green salad; fresh hot coffee or tea
$4.95

WEDNESDAY:
Savory meat loaf; golden creamed corn; hot buttered roll; choice of fresh fruit or tossed green salad; fresh hot coffee or tea
$4.25

If you cross out the adjectives in Monday's menu, you are left with a hamburger, fries, salad, and coffee or tea. These things don't sound very interesting. So restaurant owners use a lot of adjectives in their menus to make the food sound better. If the food sounds good, people might eat more.

Imagine you work at the restaurant. Describe Friday's special, which includes fish, potatoes, beans, salad, and coffee or tea.

FRIDAY: _____

_____

_____

_____

_____

When you use adjectives like *this*, *that*, *these*, and *those*, be sure they agree with the nouns they describe. When writing about one thing, use *this* or *that*.

this house
that house

When writing about two or more things, use *these* or *those*.

these houses
those houses

The word *them* is never used as an adjective. *Them* is a pronoun; never write <u>them houses</u>.

Circle the word that correctly completes each sentence.

1. We have discussed (that/those/them) problems before.
2. Look at (this/these) beautiful flower.

You are right if you chose: <u>those</u> problems, <u>this</u> flower.

A general rule to remember when using adjectives is: Keep adjectives close to the words they describe. When sentences are short, you will have no problem doing this. The adjectives are underlined in the sentences below.

<u>These</u> shoes are <u>comfortable</u>.
<u>These</u> <u>new</u> <u>black</u> shoes are <u>comfortable</u>.

But as you write longer sentences, sometimes you can accidentally put too much distance between adjectives and the noun they describe. The result can be confusing:

These shoes, I was telling my friend Sally from St. Louis, are really comfortable and lightweight.

Even such a long sentence can be made clearer if you put the noun (shoes) and its adjectives (comfortable and lightweight) closer together.

I was telling my friend Sally from St. Louis that these shoes are really comfortable and lightweight.

Underline the word that correctly completes each sentence.

1. Bring me (this/that/them) tray of food.
2. We expect him to run for re-election (this/that/those) year.
3. (This/These/Them) cars are very popular in the United States.
4. (This/These/Them) criminal charges have been dismissed.

Add adjectives to complete the sentences.

5. That man is _____.
6. Her coat looks _____.
7. The dog seems _____.
8. The student is very _____.
9. The movie was extremely _____.
10. The _____ party lasted all night.

Put an X next to the sentence that has the most adjectives.

11. ____ (1) Those two long-haired boys followed her home.
    ____ (2) Those two long-haired boys are ugly.
    ____ (3) Twenty-seven qualified persons applied for the job at the newspaper.
    ____ (4) Several applicants wanted the job, but were turned down.

12. ____ (1) There are several excellent heart specialists in town.
    ____ (2) This quaint little town has many young and competent doctors.
    ____ (3) All the doctors in town are friendly, competent, and qualified to perform heart surgery.
    ____ (4) Selma and her sister are trying to find a good doctor.

THINKING AND WRITING

1. Write a sentence that contains a list of at least three things that you own.

_____

_____

_____

2. Select one thing from the list in the sentence above. Write a sentence naming the thing. Include at least three adjectives describing it.

_____

_____

_____

3. Write one or two sentences naming persons or pets that are important to you. Use at least one adjective to describe each person or pet.

_____

_____

_____

4. Write a sentence using one of the following words as the subject: exercise, health, insurance, love.

_____

_____

_____

Compare your answers with those in *Answers and Explanations* on page 84.

STRATEGIES FOR SUCCESS

1. USING PRONOUNS INSTEAD OF NOUNS

Try not to repeat the same nouns over and over. Pronouns can make writing clearer and briefer.

STRATEGY: Check your writing.

1. Do you use the same nouns as subjects or objects too often?
2. Can pronouns be used instead of the nouns?

Example: Without pronouns, a description of a visit to the doctor might read like this:

The doctor asked how long I'd had the sore throat. The doctor said I should have called the doctor sooner. The doctor prescribed some medication and told me to take all of the medication. Then the doctor told me to come back and see the doctor again next week.

You need the noun *doctor* in the first sentence. This tells the reader who you are talking about. But the paragraph would be clearer and easier to read if the pronouns *he (she)* and *him (her)* replaced *the doctor* some of the time. The pronoun *it* could replace the noun *medication* too.

Write: Rewrite the paragraph above. Change the nouns to pronouns where you think it improves the writing.

_____

_____

_____

_____

_____

_____

2. KNOWING WHEN TO ADD ADJECTIVES

Adjectives will help the reader visualize what you are describing.

STRATEGY: Think it through.

1. Find the nouns and ask these questions about each one: WHICH?, HOW MANY?, WHAT KIND?
2. Add adjectives to answer the questions when it makes your writing clearer.

Example: The nouns in this note are underlined. What adjectives could you use to make the sentences clearer?

> *I know you'll get the job. You're a mechanic and an employee. It's a job, but you can handle it. Good luck!*

Notice how adjectives change the meaning. The writing is clearer. It's more interesting too.

> *I know you'll get that job. You're a good mechanic and a dependable employee. It's a tough job, but you can handle it. Good luck!*

Write: Underline the four nouns in the sentences below. Then rewrite the sentences, adding at least one adjective in front of each noun.

The woman was sitting at the bar, watching the door. She was waiting for her husband, who was always late.

_____

_____

_____

Compare your answers with those in *Answers and Explanations* on page 84.

Answers and Explanations

1. FINDING SUBJECTS AND OBJECTS

You can write the sentences in many ways. Here are some examples.

1. The <u>coach</u> yelled at the <u>umpire</u>.
2. <u>Connie</u> went to the <u>reunion</u>.
3. The <u>doctor</u> prescribed a strong <u>drug</u>.
4. <u>Linda</u> felt better after taking the <u>medicine</u>.
5. <u>Money</u> can't buy <u>happiness</u>.

The subjects are underlined.

6. <u>Love</u> is blind.
7. <u>Fred</u> is in love.
8. <u>Kelly</u> thinks Fred is in love with her.
9. <u>The TV station</u> is where they met.
10. <u>It</u> wasn't a very romantic first meeting.
11. But <u>Fred and Kelly</u> like to tell the story to friends.
12. <u>Their friends</u> are still surprised that they got together.
13. The common nouns are: love, station, friends.
14. The proper nouns are: Fred, Kelly.

The objects are underlined.

15. Before breakfast, Albert always reads <u>the newspaper</u>.
16. His wife would rather just stare at <u>her coffee</u>.
17. Mark lost <u>his dog</u> while walking in the park.
18. A stranger found <u>him</u>.

2. FORMING PLURALS

1. (5) is the answer. All the words are correct.
2. (3) The plural is *cookies* because you drop the *y* and add *-ies*.
3. (3) The correct plural is *gentlemen*.
4. (1) The correct plural is *roofs*.
5. processes
6. activities
7. Satellites

8. shuttles

9. rockets

10. launches

11. Companies

12. controversies

13. journeys

14. years

3. CHANGING NOUNS TO PRONOUNS

The correct pronouns are underlined.

1. You and <u>I</u> should make plans.

2. <u>We</u> girls have to stick together.

3. They want to go out with you and <u>me</u>.

4. We want to go with <u>them</u>.

5. She introduced me to <u>him</u>.

6. She went to the party with <u>him</u>.

7. <u>Yours</u> will be ready soon.

8. <u>He</u> told <u>her</u> to come along with <u>us</u>.

9. It

10. They, it

11. they

12. It

There are different ways to revise the sentences. Here are some
examples.

13. When Holly visited Susan, Susan told her she was pregnant.

14. The box broke when he dropped it on his foot.

15. His dog is always scratching his fleas.

4. USING ADJECTIVES TO CLARIFY WRITING

The correct adjective is underlined in each sentence.

1. Bring me <u>that</u> tray of food.

2. We expect him to run for re-election <u>this</u> year.

3. <u>These</u> cars are very popular in the United States.

4. <u>These</u> criminal charges have been dismissed.

There are different ways to complete sentences 5–10. Here are some examples.

5. That man is <u>fat</u>.
6. Her coat looks <u>expensive</u>.
7. The dog seems <u>friendly</u>.
8. The student is very <u>intelligent</u>.
9. The movie was extremely <u>long</u>.
10. The <u>noisy</u> party lasted all night.
11. (2) is the answer. <u>Those</u> <u>two</u> <u>long-haired</u> boys are <u>ugly</u>.
12. (2) is the answer. <u>This</u> <u>quaint</u> <u>little</u> town has <u>many</u> <u>young</u> and <u>competent</u> doctors.

THINKING AND WRITING

You can write the sentences in many ways. Here are some examples.

1. I own a car, a sofa, a dining room table, and chairs.
2. My car is a new red Toyota.
3. My family includes my beautiful wife and our young son. We have a little black dog.
4. Exercise is more important than diet.

STRATEGIES FOR SUCCESS

You can write the sentences in many ways. Here are some sample answers.

1. Using Pronouns Instead of Nouns

Your choice of pronouns depends on whether the doctor is male or female. For a female doctor, you could write:

The doctor asked how long I'd had the sore throat. <u>She</u> said I should have called <u>her</u> sooner. <u>She</u> prescribed some medication and told me to take all of <u>it</u>. Then <u>she</u> told me to come back and see <u>her</u> again next week.

2. Knowing When to Add Adjectives

The beautiful <u>woman</u> was sitting at the crowded <u>bar</u>, watching the swinging <u>door</u>. She was waiting for her elderly <u>husband</u>, who was always late.

USING VERBS AND ADVERBS

VERBS are often called action words. Verbs like *run, laugh, teach, eat,* and *reach* certainly describe actions. But words like *be, have,* and *do* are verbs too. Sometimes they stand alone. Sometimes they "help" another verb.

Good writing means using the right verbs. Verbs must give the right time information (past, present, or future). And verbs must agree with the subject (singular or plural).

Adverbs are used with verbs. Adverbs describe actions. They tell *how, when,* or *where.* Most adverbs end in *-ly,* for example, *quickly, badly,* and *honestly.*

1. VERB FORMS

Most verbs have four forms. Here are the four forms of the verb *call*.

Verb (base form)	Present Participle	Past	Past Participle
call	calling	called	called

The **base form** of any verb is the most useful. The base form is the same as the command.

<u>Call</u> when you arrive.

Use the base form when writing about *I*, *you*, or *they* in the present or future.

I <u>call</u> her every day.
You should <u>call</u> more often.
They'll <u>call</u> next week.

Add *-s* to the base form of the verb if you are writing a sentence with *he* (Ed), *she* (the woman), or *it* (her stomach) as the subject.

Ed (he) call<u>s</u> often.
She feel<u>s</u> better.
It still hurt<u>s</u> when she laugh<u>s</u>.

The present participle always ends in *-ing*. Use it to show that an action is continuing. Use it with any subject.

We'll be call<u>ing</u> you.
I'm call<u>ing</u> her now.

The past and past participle are often the same. Often, they both end in *-ed*.

BASE FORM. The simple form of the verb without any endings.

He called yesterday. (past)

I've called you several times. (past participle)

She has called you too. (past participle)

The past participle is the verb form used with a **helping verb** such as *have, has,* or *had.*

Identify the base form of each of the underlined verbs in the sentences below. Write the base form in the blanks.

1. Tom seems angry. _____
2. Sandy passed the test. _____
3. She has failed only one so far. _____
4. They are living together now. _____

Seem, pass, fail, and *live* are the base forms of the verbs in the sentences. They are all **regular verbs.** The past forms of regular verbs always end in *-ed.* The past forms of **irregular verbs** do not. Each irregular verb has its own past-tense form. The list of irregular verbs on page 88 shows the different forms for each verb.

The verbs underlined in the following sentences are irregular verbs. Write the base form of each verb in the blanks.

1. He drove as fast as he could. _____
2. It began to rain. _____
3. He has written the report. _____
4. We won! _____

Drive, begin, write, and *win* are the base forms of the verbs in the sentences.

HELPING VERB. Verbs like *have, be,* and *do* that you use with other verbs to make different tenses, questions, and negative sentences.

REGULAR VERB. A verb that you add *-ed* to when you form the past tense or the past participle.

IRREGULAR VERB. A verb that doesn't have the *-ed* ending in the past tense and past participle.

List of Irregular Verbs

BASE FORM	PAST TENSE	PAST PARTICIPLE
be	was/were	been
beat	beat	beaten
become	became	become
begin	began	begun
bend	bent	bent
bet	bet	bet
bite	bit	bitten
blow	blew	blown
break	broke	broken
bring	brought	brought
build	built	built
burst	burst	burst
buy	bought	bought
cast	cast	cast
catch	caught	caught
choose	chose	chosen
come	came	come
cost	cost	cost
creep	crept	crept
cut	cut	cut
dig	dug	dug
do	did	done
draw	drew	drawn
drink	drank	drunk
drive	drove	driven
eat	ate	eaten
fall	fell	fallen
feed	fed	fed
feel	felt	felt
fight	fought	fought
find	found	found
fit	fit	fit
fling	flung	flung
fly	flew	flown
forget	forgot	forgotten
freeze	froze	frozen
get	got	got/gotten
give	gave	given
go	went	gone
hang	hung	hung
have	had	had
hear	heard	heard
hide	hid	hidden
hit	hit	hit
hold	held	held
hurt	hurt	hurt
keep	kept	kept
know	knew	known
lay	laid	laid
lead	led	led
leave	left	left
lend	lent	lent
let	let	let

BASE FORM	PAST TENSE	PAST PARTICIPLE
lie	lay	lain
light	lit	lit
lose	lost	lost
make	made	made
mean	meant	meant
meet	met	met
put	put	put
quit	quit	quit
read	read	read
ride	rode	ridden
ring	rang	rung
rise	rose	risen
run	ran	run
say	said	said
see	saw	seen
seek	sought	sought
sell	sold	sold
send	sent	sent
set	set	set
shake	shook	shaken
shine	shone/shined	shone/shined
shoot	shot	shot
shrink	shrank/shrunk	shrunk/shrunken
shut	shut	shut
sing	sang	sung
sink	sank	sunk
sit	sat	sat
sleep	slept	slept
slide	slid	slid
speak	spoke	spoken
spend	spent	spent
stand	stood	stood
steal	stole	stolen
stick	stuck	stuck
sting	stung	stung
strike	struck	struck
swear	swore	sworn
sweep	swept	swept
swim	swam	swum
swing	swung	swung
take	took	taken
teach	taught	taught
tear	tore	torn
tell	told	told
think	thought	thought
throw	threw	thrown
understand	understood	understood
wake	woke	woke/woken
wear	wore	worn
weave	wove	woven
win	won	won
write	wrote	written

The most difficult irregular verb form to remember is the past participle. The past participle is used with a helping verb. Don't confuse it with the past tense, which can stand alone. Complete the following sentences.

1. The time has _____. (come)
2. We have just _____ to fight. (begin)
3. I haven't _____ you for so long! (see)
4. You are the best friend I have ever _____. (know)

To check your answers, look at the list of irregular verbs on page 88.

Verbs are important to a sentence. They tell WHAT is happening, and they tell WHEN it is happening (past, present, or future). When you read any sentence, you will get an idea of when the action occurs. Look at the following examples.

We <u>arrived</u> late. (past)
We usually <u>arrive</u> on time. (present)
We <u>will arrive</u> early next time. (future)

I <u>saw</u> you with her last night. (past)
I <u>see</u> a large crowd gathering. (present)
I'<u>ll</u> <u>see</u> you tomorrow. (future)

What is the tense of each of these sentences? Write <u>past</u>, <u>present</u>, or <u>future</u>.

1. They drank the whole bottle. _____
2. We gave it to Goodwill. _____
3. She takes long lunch breaks. _____
4. He'll change his mind. _____

You are right if you wrote <u>past</u> after the first two sentences, <u>present</u> after the next sentence, and <u>future</u> after the last one.

Self-Test

Answer the questions. Then compare your answers with those in *Answers and Explanations* on page 104.

In the blanks below, write the base forms of the ten verbs in these sports headlines. Then circle the one verb that is irregular.

Loughery Attacks with Bullets

Connors plays; ponders next match

Duke Defeats Kansas

Sampson Injures Back

Capitals Tie Whalers

Jordan Wins!

Ruland postpones knee surgery

Coach Resigns

Cardinals Crush LSU

1. _____
2. _____
3. _____
4. _____
5. _____
6. _____
7. _____
8. _____
9. _____
10. _____

Underline the correct form of the verb in parentheses.

11. She always (want/wants) to come along.

12. Her brother usually (say/says) no.

13. But last time she (convince/convinced) him.

14. So he (say/said/sayed) yes.

Read each sentence. Put an X next to the best way to correct the underlined part of the sentence.

15. As we stared out the window, it <u>will begin</u> to rain.
    - _____ (1) begin
    - _____ (2) begins
    - _____ (3) began
    - _____ (4) begun
    - _____ (5) No change is needed.

16. We <u>will see</u> you next week at the wedding.
    - _____ (1) see
    - _____ (2) saw
    - _____ (3) seen
    - _____ (4) have seen
    - _____ (5) No change is needed.

17. My wife <u>sleeped</u> late yesterday morning.
    - _____ (1) sleeps
    - _____ (2) sleep
    - _____ (3) will sleep
    - _____ (4) slept
    - _____ (5) No change is needed.

18. Last year her son <u>come</u> home for spring vacation.
    - _____ (1) will come
    - _____ (2) comes
    - _____ (3) came
    - _____ (4) comed
    - _____ (5) No change is needed.

2. USING HELPING VERBS

Look at the verbs in the sentences below.

I <u>am</u> ready.   (I'<u>m</u> ready.)

She <u>did</u> it.

We <u>have</u> your letter.

Sometimes the verbs *be*, *do*, and *have* stand alone, as in the sentences above.   And sometimes they "help" other verbs, as in the following sentences.

I <u>am</u> <u>hurrying</u>.   (I'<u>m</u> <u>hurrying</u>.)

She <u>did</u> <u>remember</u> the address.

We <u>have</u> <u>reviewed</u> your letter. (We'<u>ve</u> <u>reviewed</u> your letter.)

Helping verbs can be used in the past, present, or future tenses.   The chart below shows three ways to use the regular verb *play* in each tense.   The helping verbs *be*, *do*, and *have* are underlined.

Past Tense	Present Tense	Future Tense
I <u>did</u> play.	I <u>do</u> play.	I <u>will</u> play.
I <u>was</u> playing.	I <u>am</u> playing.	I <u>will</u> <u>be</u> playing.
I <u>had</u> played.	I <u>have</u> played.	I <u>will</u> <u>have</u> played.

Complete the chart using the irregular verb *write*. The first one is already done.

Past Tense	Present Tense	Future Tense
I <u>did</u> <u>write</u>.	I do _____.	I will _____.
I was _____.	I am _____.	I will be _____.
I had _____.	I have _____.	I will have _____.

The charts above show how to use the three common helping verbs.   Notice that the first line of each chart uses the base form of each verb (*play* and *write*). The second line of each chart uses the *-ing* form of each verb (*playing* and *writing*). The third line uses the past participle (*played* and *written*). Complete the following sentences with *play* and *write*.   If necessary, refer to the charts.

1. I was _____ tennis when we met.
2. I have _____ him several letters.
3. He has _____ me only once.
4. When this game is over, they will have _____ for three hours.

The helping verb *do* (did) adds emphasis to sentences. *I did call you last night* sounds more definite than *I called you last night* when answering the question *Why didn't you call me last night?*

Helping verbs are often needed when you write questions too.

Did you <u>call</u> me last night?
Aren't you <u>speaking</u> to me?
Have you <u>contacted</u> the police?
Where *did* you <u>go</u>?

FOR YOUR INFORMATION

You have read about the helping verbs *be*, *have*, and *do*. Here are some other helping verbs.

| can | would | shall | may |
| could | should | must | might |

These helping verbs can be used with one other verb.

He <u>must</u> <u>write</u> it.

Or they can be used in combination with the helping verbs *be* and *have*.

He <u>must</u> <u>be</u> <u>writing</u> it.   He <u>must</u> <u>have</u> <u>written</u> it.

Self-Test

Answer the questions. Then compare your answers with those in *Answers and Explanations* on page 104.

Use helping verbs to change the following sentences from statements to questions. The first one is already done.

1. You called me last night.

   Did you call me last night?

2. You are speaking to me.

   _____

3. You contacted the police.

   _____

4. You already ate.

   _____

5. He has been trying to get a job.

   _____

6. You have visited them before.

   _____

Choose the correct form of *be*, *have*, or *do* in parentheses. Write it in the blank.

7. _____ you think they will win the game?
   (Do, Does, Did)

8. _____ they coming with us tonight? (Am, Is, Are)

9. After today, I _____ taken the test twice.
   (will be, will have, will)

10. Tomorrow at this time, I _____ running my first
    five-mile race. (will be, will have, have been)

Underline the correct form of the verb to complete these sentences.

11. I must have (seen/saw) that movie before.
12. You should be (leaving/left) soon.
13. They can (help/helped) us.
14. He might (return/returned) tonight.

3. MATCHING THE VERB TO THE SUBJECT

You read about compound subjects in Unit 4 on page 68. All of those compound subjects were linked with the word *and*.

You <u>and</u> I make a good team.

Reading <u>and</u> writing are important communication skills.

When two parts of a compound subject are linked with the word *and*, the subject is always plural. When other linking words are used, the subject can be either plural or singular. Compound subjects are always linked with one of the following words or sets of words.

1. and
2. either . . . or
3. neither . . . nor
4. not only . . . but (also)

Look at the following sentences.

Neither Allyson nor Adam is in school now.

Not only reading but also writing is an important communication skill.

Why are singular verbs such as *am* and *is* used with these compound subjects? Because the compound subject isn't linked with *and*. When the subject isn't linked with *and*, the verb matches the part of the subject that is closest to it (Adam <u>is</u>, writing <u>is</u>).

Look at the verbs in the following sentences.

Either the newspaper or the magazines <u>are</u> on the table.

Either the magazines or the newspaper <u>is</u> on the table.

Both sentences have compound subjects. And both sets of subjects are linked with *either . . . or*. But different verbs are used. In the first sentence, the plural verb *are* matches *magazines*, the part of the subject closest to it. In the second sentence, the singular verb *is* matches *newspaper*, the part of the subject closest to it.

Underline the correct form of the verb in the following sentences.

1. Either my husband or my children (plan/plans) to attend the funeral.
2. Either my children or my husband (plan/plans) to attend the funeral.
3. Not only parks but also a swimming pool (is/are) in the neighborhood.
4. Not only a swimming pool but also parks (is/are) in the neighborhood.

If you looked at the part of the compound subject closest to the verb, you circled these words: plan, plans, is, are (children *plan*, husband *plans*, pool *is*, parks *are*).

Keep in mind the four ways that compound subjects can be linked. Watch out for sentences that seem to have compound subjects but really don't. The following two sentences are correct. Both have singular subjects. Underline the subject and circle the verb in each sentence.

1. His wife, not his children, is the beneficiary.
2. The manager, as well as all of his employees, attends the weekly meetings.

His wife and *The manager* are the subjects of the sentences. The verbs match the singular subjects (wife *is*, manager *attends*).

In some sentences, the subject comes after the verb. Some of these sentences begin with *Here* or *There*; others begin with a phrase telling WHERE. Circle the subjects in the sentences below.

1. Here comes the bride.
2. There are three bridesmaids.
3. In front of us is a beautiful sight.

4. In the balcony are the photographers, trying to be discreet.

The bride, three bridesmaids, a beautiful sight, and *the photographers* are the subjects of the sentences. The verbs match the nouns (bride *comes,* bridesmaids *are,* sight *is,* photographers *are*).

Underline the subject in each sentence below. Then circle the correct form of the verb.

1. There (is/are) problems with your account.
2. In our garden each year (grow/grows) flowers of all kinds.

The subjects and verbs of the above sentences are: problems are, flowers of all kinds grow.

Self-Test

Answer the questions. Then compare your answers with those in *Answers and Explanations* on page 105.

Underline the correct verb for each of these sentences.

1. Across the hall (is/are) two vacant apartments.

2. There (is/are) many reasons why you shouldn't go.

3. Down the street from us (live/lives) two little girls.

4. The union president, not the members, (meet/meets) with management.

5. Labor and management (work/works) together to reach an agreement.

6. Not only the members but also Jimmy (was/were) glad when it was all over.

Put an X next to the best way to correct each sentence.

7. Plato and Aristotle <u>was</u> Greek philosophers.
   - _____ (1) be
   - _____ (2) is
   - _____ (3) are
   - _____ (4) were
   - _____ (5) No change is needed.

8. Marlo Thomas, along with her parents, <u>was</u> on television last night.
   - _____ (1) be
   - _____ (2) is
   - _____ (3) are
   - _____ (4) were
   - _____ (5) No change is needed.

9. Either the veal or the steak <u>look</u> good to me.
   - _____ (1) looks
   - _____ (2) looking
   - _____ (3) has looked
   - _____ (4) have looked
   - _____ (5) No change is needed.

10. Now the Democrat, as well as the Republican, <u>is shaking hands</u> with the voters.
    - _____ (1) is shaking
    - _____ (2) are shaking hands
    - _____ (3) were shaking hands
    - _____ (4) shake hands
    - _____ (5) No change is needed.

11. Neither the mother nor her children <u>are ready</u> for summer vacation.
    - _____ (1) is ready
    - _____ (2) was ready
    - _____ (3) being ready
    - _____ (4) has been ready
    - _____ (5) No change is needed.

12. The director and the producer <u>meets</u> each week.
    - _____ (1) meet
    - _____ (2) met
    - _____ (3) meeting
    - _____ (4) meeted
    - _____ (5) No change is needed.

4. ADDING ADVERBS

Words used to describe verbs are called **adverbs**. Most adverbs end in *-ly*, and describe *how, when,* or *where*. Notice how adverbs add to the meaning of this simple sentence: She drinks.

> She drinks <u>noisily</u>.
> She drinks <u>quickly</u>.
> She <u>usually</u> drinks <u>alone</u>.

Some special adverbs, such as *very* and *somewhat,* describe other adverbs. Here is a nine-word sentence that has six adverbs:

> She <u>usually</u> drinks <u>alone</u>, <u>very</u> <u>noisily</u>, and <u>somewhat</u> <u>quickly</u>.

Add adverbs to these sentences. Use words that tell HOW and end in *-ly*.

> She always drives _____.
> He tries to dress _____.

Any word ending with *-ly* and telling HOW is an adverb. You may have written such words as *carefully* and *neatly* in the blanks.

Now look at incorrect versions of the same sentences. Why are these sentences incorrect?

> She always drives <u>careful</u>.
> He tries to dress <u>neat</u>.

The underlined words are adjectives. They can't be used to describe verbs. Remember that adjectives describe nouns; adverbs describe verbs. Adjectives could be used in the previous sentences. But you would have to write sentences like these:

> She is a <u>careful</u> driver.
> He is a <u>neat</u> dresser.

ADVERB. A word that describes a verb, an adjective, or another adverb.

Underline the adverbs in the following sentences.

1. She writes (bad/badly).
2. They danced (clumsy/clumsily) together.
3. The television blared (loud/loudly).

In all three sentences, the first word in the parentheses is an adjective. It tells WHAT KIND. The second word is an adverb telling HOW. Only adverbs (badly, clumsily, loudly) can correctly be used to describe verbs such as *writes*, *danced*, and *blared*.

Adverbs, unlike adjectives, can be placed almost anywhere in a sentence. The meaning is the same in all the sentences below. All are correct.

<u>Slowly</u>, the old man edged up to the counter.
The old man edged up to the counter <u>slowly</u>.
The old man <u>slowly</u> edged up to the counter.

Write the following sentence in three ways. Each time, put the adverb *loudly* in a different place in the sentence.

They laughed at his jokes.

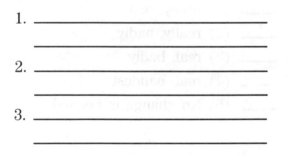

1. _____
   _____
2. _____
   _____
3. _____
   _____

Loudly can be the first or last word of the sentence. If it's the first word, you have to put a comma after it (Loudly,). Also, *loudly* can go on either side of the verb *laughed*.

Self-Test

Answer the questions. Then compare your answers with those in *Answers and Explanations* on page 105.

Put an X next to the best way to correct the sentences.

1. Thoroughly and complete, the reporter investigates each lead.
   - _____ (1) Thorough and complete
   - _____ (2) Thoroughly and completely
   - _____ (3) Thorough and completely
   - _____ (4) Thoroughly complete
   - _____ (5) No change is needed.

2. She answered his questions quick and nervous.
   - _____ (1) quickly nervous
   - _____ (2) quickly and nervous
   - _____ (3) quick and nervously
   - _____ (4) quickly and nervously
   - _____ (5) No change is needed.

3. "Turn off those TV cameras immediately," she demanded angrily.
   - _____ (1) immediately, angry
   - _____ (2) immediate, angry
   - _____ (3) immediate, angrier
   - _____ (4) immediate, angrily
   - _____ (5) No change is needed.

4. The news director cautious and deliberately reviewed the story before it went on the air.
   - _____ (1) cautiously and deliberately
   - _____ (2) cautiously deliberate
   - _____ (3) cautious and deliberate
   - _____ (4) deliberately cautious
   - _____ (5) No change is needed.

5. Since the severely accident, she speaks very slowly.
   - _____ (1) very severely, slowly
   - _____ (2) severe, slow
   - _____ (3) severe, slowly
   - _____ (4) severely, slow
   - _____ (5) No change is needed.

6. I'm real afraid I scored bad on the test.
   - _____ (1) really, bad
   - _____ (2) really, badly
   - _____ (3) real, badly
   - _____ (4) real, baddest
   - _____ (5) No change is needed.

THINKING AND WRITING

1. Write three to four sentences about your work experience. Use the past tense as well as helping verbs and past participles. If you need help getting started, you can begin: "During the past year, I have . . ."

_____

_____

_____

_____

_____

_____

_____

2. Write two or three sentences about your goals for the coming year. Use the present and future tenses. Try to use the contraction *I'll* at least once.

_____

_____

_____

_____

3. Add as many adverbs as you can to these sentences. Underline the adverbs.

a. She sings.

_____

b. They fought.

_____

c. He slept.

_____

Compare your answers with those in *Answers and Explanations* on page 105.

STRATEGIES FOR SUCCESS

1. USING THE RIGHT VERB FORM

Be sure the verbs you use match the subject and the time.

STRATEGY: Check your writing.

1. Identify the subject and the time.
2. Watch for the helping verb *have*.

Example: Imagine you've written these sentences and you're not sure if the underlined verbs are correct.

On our vacation, we <u>ran</u> into some old friends. We hadn't <u>saw</u> them since we all went to a disco together six years ago. We <u>lose</u> contact with them until this year.

We is the subject of all the sentences. The time is the past. *Ran* is correct in the first sentence. But the next verb follows the helping verb *had*. So you need to use the past participle *seen*. *Lose* is a present-tense verb in a sentence about the past. So *lost* is the correct form here.

Write: Rewrite the paragraph below. Be sure the verbs match the subjects and the time of the action. Be sure past participles follow the helping verb *have*.

We'll all been ready to go soon. We've be looking forward to this trip for weeks. We haven't took a vacation in two years. Last time we go to the ocean. We haven't go anywhere since.

_____

_____

_____

_____

_____

2. ADDING WORDS TO DESCRIBE ACTIONS

Adverbs help the reader picture more clearly what you are writing about.

STRATEGY: Think it through.

1. Identify the action words.
2. Add words that tell HOW, WHEN, or WHERE.

Example: The passage below has no adverbs. What words might make the sentences clearer and more precise?

He was brought to trial. At first, he had answered questions. He didn't want to be accused of the crime.

The verbs in the sentences are *brought, answered, want, be,* and *accused.* You could write the following:

He was <u>finally</u> brought to trial. At first, he had answered questions <u>willingly</u> and <u>honestly</u>. He didn't want to be <u>unjustly</u> accused of the crime.

Write: Rewrite the following sentences. Add adverbs where they can help make the sentences clearer and more precise.

He protested. He denied his guilt. Then he gave up and confessed.

_____

_____

_____

_____

_____

Compare your answers with those in *Answers and Explanations* on page 106.

Answers and Explanations

1. VERB FORMS

1. attack
2. play
3. ponder
4. defeat
5. injure
6. tie
7. win
8. postpone
9. resign
10. crush

The irregular verb is *win*.

11. She always <u>wants</u> to come along.
12. Her brother usually <u>says</u> no.
13. But last time she <u>convinced</u> him.
14. So he <u>said</u> yes.
15. (3) began
16. (5) No change is needed.
17. (4) slept
18. (3) came

2. USING HELPING VERBS

There are many ways to answer the questions. Here are some examples.

2. Are you speaking to me?
3. Did you contact the police?
4. Have you already eaten? (Have you eaten already?)
5. Has he been trying to get a job?
6. Have we visited them before?
7. <u>Do</u> you think they will win the game?
8. <u>Are</u> they coming with us tonight?
9. After today, I <u>will have</u> taken the test twice.
10. Tomorrow at this time, I <u>will be</u> running my first five-mile race.
11. I must have <u>seen</u> that movie before.
12. You should be <u>leaving</u> soon.

13. They can <u>help</u> us.

14. He might <u>return</u> tonight.

3. MATCHING THE VERB TO THE SUBJECT

1. Across the hall <u>are</u> two vacant apartments.

2. There <u>are</u> many reasons why you shouldn't go.

3. Down the street from us <u>live</u> two little girls.

4. The union president, not the members, <u>meets</u> with management.

5. Labor and management <u>work</u> together to reach an agreement.

6. Not only the members but also Jimmy <u>was</u> glad when it was all over.

7. (4) were

8. (5) No change is needed.

9. (1) looks

10. (5) No change is needed.

11. (5) No change is needed.

12. (1) meet

4. ADDING ADVERBS

1. (2) Thoroughly and completely

2. (4) quickly and nervously

3. (5) No change is needed.

4. (1) cautiously and deliberately

5. (3) severe, slowly

6. (2) really, badly

THINKING AND WRITING

You can answer the questions in many ways. Here are some examples. In the first answer, helping verbs, past participles, and past-tense verbs are underlined.

1.　　During the past, I <u>have worked</u> as a waitress and a nurse's aide. I <u>worked</u> as a waitress for three months. Then I <u>found out</u> about the other job, which pays better. I <u>have been</u> a nurse's aide for six months now.

2.   During the next year, I hope to get my degree. I'll also take some kind of vacation. Then I plan to look for a new job.

3. a. She <u>usually</u> sings <u>very</u> <u>beautifully</u>.
   b. They <u>often</u> fought <u>loudly</u>.
   c. He slept <u>soundly</u> and <u>peacefully</u>.

STRATEGIES FOR SUCCESS

1. Using the Right Verb Form

We'll all <u>be</u> ready to go soon. We've <u>been</u> looking forward to this trip for weeks. We haven't <u>taken</u> a vacation in two years. Last time we <u>went</u> to the ocean. We haven't <u>gone</u> anywhere since.

2. Adding Words to Describe Actions

You can answer this question in many ways. Here are some of the adverbs you could use.

He protested <u>strongly</u>. He <u>loudly</u> denied his guilt. Then <u>suddenly</u> he gave up and <u>tearfully</u> confessed.

CORRECTING YOUR SPELLING

EVEN the best writing will make a poor impression if words are spelled wrong. In this unit, you'll learn several rules that will help you spell correctly.

General spelling rules, such as those that tell you how to add endings to words, can save time. But some words give us special problems. They sound alike but have different spellings and meanings. It's important to learn these words.

This unit will show you how to use a dictionary too. The dictionary is the best place to check the spelling of words you don't know.

1. WORDS THAT SOUND ALIKE

<u>Who's</u> that at the door?

<u>It's</u> your husband!

<u>We're</u> trying to get in!

<u>They're</u> following us.

<u>You're</u> kidding!

The words underlined above are contractions. All of them are spelled correctly. They're abbreviated versions of the following words.

who is

it is

we are

they are

you are

If you replace a contraction with the two words from the list above, the meaning is the same. Then you know the word is spelled correctly.

Now look at these words.

whose

its

were

their, there

your

These words sound the same as the contractions used above. But they're spelled differently. And they have different meanings. For example, *its*, *their*, and *your* are possessive pronouns, not contractions. Here are those same words, used correctly in sentences.

<u>Whose</u> sweater is this?

The dog wagged <u>its</u> tail.

Where <u>were</u> you?

<u>Their</u> tickets are <u>there</u> on the bookshelf.

Is this <u>your</u> idea of a joke?

How do you know whether to use a contraction or a possessive pronoun in a sentence? The rule is: Use the contraction only if you can replace the word with two words. For example, you know that these underlined words are spelled correctly after you try to replace them with two words:

"<u>Who's</u> at the door?" can be changed to "<u>Who</u> <u>is</u> at the door?" "<u>Whose</u> sweater is this?" can't be changed to "<u>Who</u> <u>is</u> sweater is this?"

Apply the same test and underline the correct words in the sentences below.

1. (Were/We're) ready.
2. Get (your/you're) coat.
3. (Its/It's) late, and (its/it's) time to leave.
4. (Their/They're) starting (their/they're) vacation today.

Sentences 1, 3, and 4 need contractions. Use possessive pronouns only to describe *your* coat in sentence 2 and *their* vacation in sentence 4.

Words that sound alike but have different meanings and usually different spellings are called **homonyms.** Here is a list of some common homonyms. Notice the different spellings and meanings.

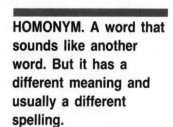

HOMONYM. A word that sounds like another word. But it has a different meaning and usually a different spelling.

hour—60 minutes	be— a verb: "*Be* quiet!"
our—belonging to us	bee—an insect
meet—to come together	know—to understand
meat—flesh	no—the opposite of yes

piece—a part

peace—the opposite of
war

red—a color

read—the past tense of
read: "I read it yes-
terday."

right—correct

right—the opposite of left

right—a privilege

write—to put on paper

sail—to travel by boat

sale—a bargain

weight—the amount
something weighs

wait—to pass time

whole—entire

hole—an opening

pane—a piece of glass in a window

pain—hurt

sea—a body of water

see—to look

to—"I want *to* help."

too—also

two—2

through—"We went *through*
a tunnel."

threw—the past tense of
throw: "He *threw* the ball."

sew—to stitch

so—therefore

weigh—to measure weight

way—a manner; a direction

would—"*Would* you come with me?"

wood—a material from trees

Underline the correct words to complete the sentences below.   Check your answers against the list of homonyms above and on the previous page.

1. We can't (sea/see) the (sea/see) from here.
2. Did you (sew/so) that dress yourself?
3. Do you (know/no) the (way/weigh) to San Jose?
4. Matthew (rights/writes) very well.

Self-Test

Underline the word that correctly completes each sentence.

1. She is (right/write), and he is wrong.
2. Do you (know/no) of any job openings?
3. (Your/You're) late!
4. (Their/There/They're) coming soon.
5. He (read/red) the article yesterday.
6. (Its/It's) good to (meat/meet) you.

Put an X next to the sentence that has no spelling errors.

7. ____ (1) Wood you be interested in a new job?
   ____ (2) I no of one at the brewery.
   ____ (3) Were looking for a new supervisor.
   ____ (4) Ours quit last Friday.

8. ____ (1) You two guys are trying to do too much.
   ____ (2) You too guys are trying too do to much.
   ____ (3) You to guys are trying to do too much.
   ____ (4) You two guys are trying too do two much.

9. ____ (1) Well be able to see the results soon.
   ____ (2) We'll be able to sea the results soon.
   ____ (3) Well bee able to see the results soon.
   ____ (4) We'll be able to see the results soon.

10. ____ (1) They're planning too meet us their later.
    ____ (2) They're planning to meet us there later.
    ____ (3) Their planning too meet us there later.
    ____ (4) Their planning to meat us there later.

11. ____ (1) Your so right!
    ____ (2) Your sew right!
    ____ (3) Your so write!
    ____ (4) You're so right!

12. ____ (1) Who's going to be there?
    ____ (2) Who's going too be their?
    ____ (3) Whose going to be their?
    ____ (4) Whose going to be there?

2. RULES YOU CAN USE

The "*i* before *e*" rule is one of the most helpful spelling rules. A short **rhyme** will help you remember the specifics:

I before *e*,

except after *c*,

and when sounded as *a*

as in *neighbor* and *weigh*.

Here are some familiar examples of "*i* before *e*."

pi<u>e</u>ce   pi<u>e</u>   fri<u>e</u>nd

But when those two letters follow a *c*, the *e* comes first.

rec<u>ei</u>ve   rec<u>ei</u>pt   dec<u>ei</u>ve

And the *e* comes first in words that have the *a* sound.

fr<u>ei</u>ght   sl<u>ei</u>gh   w<u>ei</u>ght

Here are some exceptions to the "*i* before *e*" rule.

<u>ei</u>ther	h<u>ei</u>ght	anc<u>ie</u>nt
n<u>ei</u>ther	l<u>ei</u>sure	spec<u>ie</u>s
for<u>ei</u>gn	s<u>ei</u>ze	sc<u>ie</u>nce
forf<u>ei</u>t	w<u>ei</u>rd	consc<u>ie</u>nce

You might want to try to memorize the spelling of these words.

Circle the misspelled words in the sentences below. Rewrite the words correctly in the blanks.

1. She gave her freind a piece
   of pie.   _____

2. You can't return that sleigh
   without a sales reciept.   _____

3. List your hieght and wieght
   on the application form.   _____

Here are some rules to use when you add endings to words. These rules apply to all endings that start with a vowel, such as *-ing, -ed, -er,* and *-est.*

With most words, such as those listed below, just add the ending.

start	+	-ed	=	started
feel	+	-ing	=	feeling
remind	+	-er	=	reminder
nice	+	-est	=	nicest

Notice that if a word ends in *e* (nice), you drop the *e* before you add the ending.

When you have a three- or four-letter word that has one vowel in the middle, the rule is: Double the last letter and add the ending.

hop	+	-ing	=	hopping
fit	+	-ed	=	fitted
fat	+	-er	=	fatter
flat	+	-est	=	flattest

The same rule applies to longer words that have the **accent** on the last **syllable** of the word.

admit	+	-ed	=	admitted
begin	+	-ing	=	beginning

As with all rules, there are always exceptions. So if the spelling of a word looks strange to you, look it up in a dictionary.

ACCENT. The emphasis you put on one part of a word.

SYLLABLE. One or more letters in a word that make up a separate sound, for example, syl-la-ble.

Underline the word that correctly completes each sentence.

1. Drug use seems to increase as Americans have more (leisure/liesure) time.

2. Some of the secrets of (anceint/ancient) times are only now being discovered.

3. Medical (sceince/science) has progressed greatly during the past decade.

4. The American dollar is worth more than most (foreign/foriegn) currency.

5. He is (copping/coping) with his wife's illness, but the days seem long.

6. The reviewers (ratted/rated) the restaurant highly.

Put an X next to the sentence that has no spelling errors.

7. ___ (1) Neither Mae nor Florence is coming to work today.

___ (2) Mae's consceince is bothering her.

___ (3) She was caught stealing yesterday.

___ (4) They found her in the frieght car.

8. ___ (1) Mae always did seem a little wierd to the rest of us.

___ (2) She was quieter than most, always keeping to herself.

___ (3) Still, we were shocked when they siezed her with the goods.

___ (4) She would have recieved her first paycheck today.

9. ___ (1) The event was upsetting to everyone.

___ (2) Florence blamed herself for not stoping Mae.

___ (3) We told her that controling other people is never easy.

___ (4) But she still regreted that she recommended Mae for the job.

10. ___ (1) We're hopping nothing like this will ever happen again.

___ (2) We're all feelling foolish.

___ (3) No one likes to be decieved.

___ (4) It's something that weighs on your mind for a long time.

11. ___ (1) Mo was tapping a television program on his VCR.

___ (2) Suddenly he heard a taping sound on the window.

___ (3) He was hopping it was only the wind.

___ (4) And that's what it turned out to be.

12. ___ (1) Brigitte is one of the finest cooks I know.

___ (2) While stiring the soup, she spoke about her past.

___ (3) She learnned to cook from her German mother.

___ (4) Now she is startting to teach her children some of her secrets.

3. USING THE DICTIONARY

You may have heard people mention the dictionary as a good spelling aid. But one good question is, "If I don't know how to spell a word, how can I look it up in a dictionary?" There are two things you can do.

1. Write down all the possible spellings of a word. Then look up each of the spellings until you find the right one.
2. Look for the word listed under a different word.

For example, imagine you have written the two sentences below. You think that you may have misspelled the words that are underlined.

1. I got <u>payed</u> today.

2. I need your <u>anser</u> as soon as possible.

What are some possible spellings of the underlined words?

1. a. payed
   b. paid
   c. pade

2. a. anser
   b. ansser

Pretend you wrote the lists above. Your next step is to look up what you think is most likely to be the correct spelling of the word. If you are right the first time, you will save time.

Sometimes an easier way to check your spelling is to look for the word listed under a different word. For example, you could look up the word *pay*, which is the base form of the word *paid*. There you will find the past tense.

pay (pā) *v.* **paid, paying, pays.** —*tr.* **1.** To give money in exchange for goods or services. **2.** To get revenge for; to punish. Often used with *back* or *off: I paid him back for his rudeness.* **3.** To bear the cost of: *He paid my way through school.*

If you have trouble remembering the spelling for a word like *answer*, you can look up other words with the same meaning, such as *reply* or *respond*.

> **re·ply** (rĭ-plī') *v.* **-plied, -plying, -plies** —*intr.* **1.** To answer in speech or writing. **2.** To respond by some action or gesture: *He replied by nodding his head.* **3.** To echo. **4.** *Law.* To answer a defendant's plea. —*tr.* To say or give as an answer: *He replied that he wasn't guilty.* —See Synonyms at (answer.)

> **re·spond** (rĭ-spŏnd') *v.* **-sponded, -sponding, -sponds.** —*intr.* **1.** To answer. **2.** To reply. **3.** To react positively. —*tr.* To say in reply; to answer. —See Synonyms at (answer.)

Any time you look up a word in the dictionary, you have to use your knowledge of the alphabet. All the words in the dictionary are **in alphabetical order.** This is also true about almost any word list, including the **glossary** in this book and the names in the telephone book.

You know that the word *among* comes before the word *weird* in the dictionary. Look at the two pairs of words below. Put a check next to the one that would come first in the dictionary.

1. ____ misspell
   ____ necessary

2. ____ quotation
   ____ repetition

If two words start with different letters, you just look at the first letter of each. You'll notice which letter comes first in the alphabet. You probably checked *misspell* and *quotation* as the correct answers above.

But what if two or more words begin with the same letter? You then look at the second letter to see which comes first in the alphabet. So *a* in *sandwich* comes before *y* in *syllable*. And *e* in *perform* comes before *r* in *professor*.

If two words start with the same two letters, you look at the third letter, and so on. So *definition* comes before *develop*. And *commissioner* comes before *committee*.

IN ALPHABETICAL ORDER. Arranged in the order of the letters of the alphabet (a, b, c, d, etc.).

GLOSSARY. A list of the glosses in a book. A *gloss* is a brief explanation like the ones in the margins of this book.

Look at the two lists of words below. Put a check beside the word in each list that would come first in the dictionary. Then check your answers by looking up the words in the word list on pages 118 and 119.

1. _____ lose   2. _____ meant
   _____ losing   _____ marriage
   _____ leisure   _____ mathematics

Good spelling takes practice. Using the dictionary is an important part of that practice. Good spellers are able to spot spelling mistakes. They may not know how to spell every word. But they know when a word "looks wrong." Then they try to rewrite the word correctly, or they look it up to find the correct spelling.

Look at the *200 Commonly Misspelled Words* on the next two pages. Study them a few at a time. Soon you'll be able to spell these difficult words correctly. Also, look up one or two of the unfamiliar words every day. This will give you practice in using the dictionary.

After you have studied the *200 Commonly Misspelled Words*, complete the exercise below. It will show you if you're developing the ability to spot spelling errors.

Check the misspelled word in each set. Then write the correct spelling in the blank.

1. _____ cafeteria   2. _____ appreciate   3. _____ absense
   _____   _____   _____
   _____ calender   _____ discipline   _____ bicycle
   _____   _____   _____
   _____ changeable   _____ intresting   _____ controlled
   _____   _____   _____

200 COMMONLY MISSPELLED WORDS

A
absence
accidentally
acquaintance
across
already
among
analyze
answer
anxious
appearance
appreciate
approximately
argument
arrangement
article
athletic
awkward

B
beginning
belief
believe
benefit
bicycle
bulletin
business

C
cafeteria
calendar
campaign
cancel
certain
changeable
choose
clothes
coming
committee
completely
conscience
conscious
consequences
controlled
convenience
corporation
courageous
criticism
cylinder

D
deceive
defendant
definition
describe
description
desert
desirable
dessert
develop
development
different
disappear
disappoint
disapprove
discipline

E
especially
embarrass
emphasize
exaggerate
excellent
experience
extremely

F
familiar
finally
forty
fourth
freight

G
generally
government
governor
grammar
guarantee

H
height
hungry
humorous

I
icicle
immediately
immense
incidentally
indefinite
independent
inquiries
intelligent
interesting
interfere

J
judge

K
knowledge

L
laboratory
leisure
library
loneliness
loose
lose
losing

M
marriage
mathematics
meant
minute
misspell
mortgage

N
necessary
niece
ninety
noticeable

O
occasion
occurred
occurring
omitted
opinion
opportunity
ordinarily
original

P

paid
peculiar
perform
performance
perhaps
permanent
personal
personnel
persuade
physician
piece
planned
politician
preferred
prejudice
principal
principle
privilege
probably
pronunciation

Q

questionnaire
quotation

R

realize
really
receipt
receive
recognize
recommend
recommendation
reference
referred
relieve
religious

repetition
reputation
restaurant
rhythm
ridiculous

S

sandwich
schedule
secretary
sense
separate
separation
shining
similar
sincerely
sophomore
speech
straight
studying
succeed
success
superintendent
supervisor
surely
surprise
suspicion

T

technical
temporarily
thermometer
thoroughly
through
toaster
together
tolerable
tried

typewriting
typical

U

unconscious
until
useful
usually
utilities

V

valuable
various
vegetable
vehicle

W

weather
whether
woman
wrestle
writing
written

Self-Test

In each set of words, put an X next to the misspelled word if there is one. If there is no misspelled word, put an X next to number (5).

1. ____ (1) embarrass
   ____ (2) tried
   ____ (3) opinion
   ____ (4) necesary
   ____ (5) no error

5. ____ (1) orignal
   ____ (2) icicle
   ____ (3) bicycle
   ____ (4) library
   ____ (5) no error

9. ____ (1) either
   ____ (2) neither
   ____ (3) height
   ____ (4) weight
   ____ (5) no error

2. ____ (1) misspell
   ____ (2) omited
   ____ (3) describe
   ____ (4) certain
   ____ (5) no error

6. ____ (1) extremely
   ____ (2) knowledge
   ____ (3) tecnical
   ____ (4) judge
   ____ (5) no error

10. ____ (1) dessert
    ____ (2) religious
    ____ (3) probably
    ____ (4) generaly
    ____ (5) no error

3. ____ (1) benefit
   ____ (2) wresle
   ____ (3) criticism
   ____ (4) especially
   ____ (5) no error

7. ____ (1) until
   ____ (2) useful
   ____ (3) usually
   ____ (4) exagerate
   ____ (5) no error

11. ____ (1) occasion
    ____ (2) occurred
    ____ (3) preferred
    ____ (4) occuring
    ____ (5) no error

4. ____ (1) fourty
   ____ (2) fourth
   ____ (3) friend
   ____ (4) finally
   ____ (5) no error

8. ____ (1) conceive
   ____ (2) deceive
   ____ (3) across
   ____ (4) receive
   ____ (5) no error

12. ____ (1) disapprove
    ____ (2) payed
    ____ (3) prejudice
    ____ (4) experience
    ____ (5) no error

THINKING AND WRITING

1. Pretend the sentence below is part of an announcement you are writing. Add two or three sentences to complete the announcement. Use contractions and words with endings (-*ed*, -*ing*, etc.) as much as possible. Check your spelling.

Our neighborhood picnic is scheduled for May 4.

2. Look at the following words. If you are unsure of the meanings of some of them, look them up in a dictionary.

personal	preferred
personnel	principal
persuade	principle
planned	probably

Write three or four sentences, using as many of these words as you can.

Compare your answers with those in *Answers and Explanations* on page 125.

STRATEGIES FOR SUCCESS

1. SPOTTING SPELLING PROBLEMS

Get your ideas down on paper before you worry about your spelling. Then go back and check words that look wrong.

STRATEGY: Recheck words that don't look right.

1. Look them over.
2. Talk them out.

Example: Imagine you're writing a letter and you need to recheck the underlined words. Look over the words in the first sentence. Do you think they're correct? Talk out the words in the second sentence. Are contractions needed?

The food wasn't <u>familure</u>, but it was <u>intresting</u>. <u>Your</u> right; <u>its</u> a great place to get a cheap meal.

When you look over "familure" and "intresting," you discover that each word has a missing letter or sound. When you talk out "your" and "its," say "you are" and "it is" instead. So you realize you should use the contractions *you're* and *it's*.

Write: Imagine you're applying for a job. You plan to recheck the underlined words in your letter for spelling.

<u>You're</u> ad for shop foreman <u>intrested</u> me. <u>Its</u> the kind of job <u>I'd</u> like. <u>I'm</u> well <u>qualfied</u> to do that kind of work.

Look over the words "intrested" and "qualfied." What are some other ways you could spell them?

1. intrested   2. qualfied

_____   _____

_____   _____

Now circle the spellings you think are correct.

Talk out the other words in the paragraph on page 122. Then rewrite the two words that should be changed.

3. _____   4. _____

2. USING THE DICTIONARY

Sometimes, using the dictionary is the only way to be sure your spelling is correct.

STRATEGY: Look it up.
1. Look up the word as you think it is spelled.
2. Look up a similar word.

Example: Underline the four misspelled words below. How can you find their correct spellings in the dictionary?

I'm writting to accspress my simpathy over the passing of your husbund.

You can find the correct word *writing* by looking up *write* or *writing*. *Express* may be hard to find if you don't know it starts with *ex-*. But you might find it if you look up *say* or *tell*. *Sympathy* is also listed in the dictionary under *sorry*. You can find *husband* easily because the first four letters are correct.

Write: Underline the four misspelled words in the sentences below. Use the dictionary to find the correct spellings. Write the correct words in the blanks.

We'll be comming home for Christmas. We tride to call you last night. We'll probibly stay at a motell.

1. _____   3. _____
2. _____   4. _____

Compare your answers with those in *Answers and Explanations* on page 125.

Answers and Explanations

1. WORDS THAT SOUND ALIKE

1. She is <u>right</u>, and he is wrong.
2. Do you <u>know</u> of any job openings?
3. <u>You're</u> late!
4. <u>They're</u> coming soon.
5. He <u>read</u> the article yesterday.
6. <u>It's</u> good to <u>meet</u> you.

7. (4) is correct.
8. (1) is correct.
9. (4) is correct.
10. (2) is correct.
11. (4) is correct.
12. (1) is correct.

2. RULES YOU CAN USE

1. Drug use seems to increase as Americans have more <u>leisure</u> time.
2. Some of the secrets of <u>ancient</u> times are only now being discovered.
3. Medical <u>science</u> has progressed greatly during the past decade.
4. The American dollar is worth more than most <u>foreign</u> currency.
5. He is <u>coping</u> with his wife's illness, but the days seem long.
6. The reviewers <u>rated</u> the restaurant highly.
7. (1) is correct.
8. (2) is correct.
9. (1) is correct.
10. (4) is correct.
11. (4) is correct.
12. (1) is correct.

3. USING THE DICTIONARY

1. (4) The correct spelling is *necessary*.
2. (2) The correct spelling is *omitted*.
3. (2) The correct spelling is *wrestle*.
4. (1) The correct spelling is *forty*.
5. (1) The correct spelling is *original*.
6. (3) The correct spelling is *technical*.
7. (4) The correct spelling is *exaggerate*.
8. (5) There is no error.

9. (5) There is no error.

10. (4) The correct spelling is *generally*.

11. (4) The correct spelling is *occurring*.

12. (2) The correct spelling is *paid*.

THINKING AND WRITING

You can answer the questions in many ways. Here are some sample answers.

1.   Our neighborhood picnic is scheduled for May 4. We've all worked hard in organizing this event. We're hoping everyone in the neighborhood can come. We plan to eat at noon. Contests and games are planned for later. It's going to be an exciting time. We'll see you there!

2.   The personnel director said that the school principal planned to resign for personal reasons. It was probably a matter of principle. He preferred to look for another field of study. No one could persuade him to change his mind.

STRATEGIES FOR SUCCESS

1. Spotting Spelling Problems

1. interested
2. qualified
3. your
4. It's

2. Using the Dictionary

1. coming
2. tried
3. probably
4. motel

Check What You've Learned

Check What You've Learned will give you an idea of how well you've learned the writing skills in this book. This test consists of 36 questions similar to those on the GED Test.

Read each question carefully. Then put an X next to the BEST answer. There is no time limit.

CAPITALIZATION

Put an X next to the underlined part of the sentence that is NOT correct. If there is no error, mark number (5).

1. Why can't i come with you to the museum?
   - _____ (1) Why
   - _____ (2) i
   - _____ (3) you
   - _____ (4) museum
   - _____ (5) no error

2. Thanksgiving Day is always the fourth Thursday of November.
   - _____ (1) Thanksgiving
   - _____ (2) Day
   - _____ (3) Thursday
   - _____ (4) November
   - _____ (5) no error

3. His birthday is in February, the same Month as mine.
   - _____ (1) His
   - _____ (2) birthday
   - _____ (3) February
   - _____ (4) Month
   - _____ (5) no error

4. Forty-eight-year-old Dan Greenburg wrote a book called Confessions Of a Pregnant Father.
   - _____ (1) Of
   - _____ (2) a
   - _____ (3) Pregnant
   - _____ (4) Father
   - _____ (5) no error

PUNCTUATION

Put an X next to the underlined part of the sentence that is NOT correct. If there is no error, mark number (5).

5. <u>Does</u> <u>Sam's</u> boss know why <u>he's</u> acting so strangely<u>.</u>
   - ____ (1) Does
   - ____ (2) Sam's
   - ____ (3) he's
   - ____ (4) .
   - ____ (5) no error

6. <u>Does</u> he think <u>I'm</u> after <u>his</u> job<u>?</u>
   - ____ (1) Does
   - ____ (2) I'm
   - ____ (3) his
   - ____ (4) ?
   - ____ (5) no error

7. <u>Your</u> <u>our</u> first choice so far, but <u>we'll</u> be interviewing <u>others</u> this afternoon.
   - ____ (1) Your
   - ____ (2) our
   - ____ (3) we'll
   - ____ (4) others
   - ____ (5) no error

8. <u>His</u> <u>coat's</u> collar is frayed, but <u>her's</u> <u>isn't</u>.
   - ____ (1) His
   - ____ (2) coat's
   - ____ (3) her's
   - ____ (4) isn't
   - ____ (5) no error

Put an X next to the sentence that is punctuated correctly.

9. ____ (1) Committee members talked with Harry, Pat, Ben, Sue, and Al.

   ____ (2) Committee members, talked with Harry, Pat, Ben, Sue and Al.

   ____ (3) Committee members talked with, Harry, Pat, Ben, Sue and Al.

   ____ (4) Committee members talked with Harry Pat Ben Sue and Al.

   ____ (5) None of the sentences are correct.

SENTENCES

Put an X next to the group of words that is NOT a correct and complete sentence. If all the sentences are correct, mark number (5).

10. ____ (1) He is a junior in high school.
____ (2) He's a junior.
____ (3) She attended a junior college for two years.
____ (4) An educational institution offering a two-year course.
____ (5) All are complete sentences.

11. ____ (1) Iran used to be called Persia.
____ (2) Iran is still an important supplier of oil to other countries.
____ (3) Persia was an ancient country in southwestern Asia.
____ (4) Persia was renamed Iran in 1935.
____ (5) All are complete sentences.

12. ____ (1) We expect them, to approve the contract, then we'll get our money.
____ (2) We expect them.
____ (3) We expect them to approve the contract then.
____ (4) We expect them to approve the contract.
____ (5) All are complete sentences.

Put an X next to the best way to change each group of words into a complete sentence. Mark number (5) if no change is needed.

13. After getting his real estate license.
____ (1) Add the words he began earning money.
____ (2) Add the words which required much studying.
____ (3) Take away the words real estate license.
____ (4) Take away the word After.
____ (5) No change is needed.

14. Because it was very late.

　_____ (1) Add the words and the weather was terrible.

　_____ (2) Add the words and everyone was very tired.

　_____ (3) Take away the word Because.

　_____ (4) Take away the word very.

　_____ (5) No change is needed.

15. Are you ready?

　_____ (1) Add the words to go.

　_____ (2) Add the word now.

　_____ (3) Take away the word Are.

　_____ (4) Take away the word ready.

　_____ (5) No change is needed.

16. He always try to see the bright side of every situation.

　_____ (1) Change He to She.

　_____ (2) Change try to tries.

　_____ (3) Change every to all.

　_____ (4) Take away the words of every situation.

　_____ (5) No change is needed.

NOUNS, PRONOUNS, AND ADJECTIVES

Four words are underlined in each of the following sentences. If an error is underlined, put an X next to the number. If there is no error, mark number (5).

17. Three mouses were found in houses in this neighborhood last week.

　_____ (1) mouses

　_____ (2) houses

　_____ (3) neighborhood

　_____ (4) week

　_____ (5) no error

18. The leaves have collected in the gutters and on the roofs.

　_____ (1) leaves

　_____ (2) collected

　_____ (3) gutters

　_____ (4) roofs

　_____ (5) no error

19. He knew she would agree to come with he and his family.

　_____ (1) He

　_____ (2) she

　_____ (3) he

　_____ (4) his

　_____ (5) no error

20. They asked I several days ago if it was OK for him to join the group.

　_____ (1) They

　_____ (2) I

　_____ (3) it

　_____ (4) him

　_____ (5) no error

21. The <u>music</u> was <u>loudly</u>, but we could still understand some of the <u>familiar</u> <u>lyrics</u>.
    _____ (1) music
    _____ (2) loudly
    _____ (3) familiar
    _____ (4) lyrics
    _____ (5) no error

22. The <u>solution</u> is <u>simple</u>: find the <u>sneaky</u> <u>culprit</u> and punish him.
    _____ (1) solution
    _____ (2) simple
    _____ (3) sneaky
    _____ (4) culprit
    _____ (5) no error

23. <u>My</u> <u>grandfather</u> outlived <u>four</u> <u>wifes</u>.
    _____ (1) My
    _____ (2) grandfather
    _____ (3) four
    _____ (4) wifes
    _____ (5) no error

VERBS AND ADVERBS

Four words or phrases are underlined in each of the following sentences. If an error is underlined, put an X next to the number. If there is no error, mark number (5).

24. Phil <u>seem</u> <u>surprised</u> to <u>hear</u> that Shirley had <u>passed</u> the test.
    _____ (1) seem
    _____ (2) surprised
    _____ (3) hear
    _____ (4) passed
    _____ (5) no error

25. She <u>said</u> the cat <u>have</u> <u>eaten</u> our <u>pet</u> bird.
    _____ (1) said
    _____ (2) have
    _____ (3) eaten
    _____ (4) pet
    _____ (5) no error

26. Martha will <u>be</u> ready by the time Frank <u>has</u> <u>finish</u> <u>dressing</u>.
    _____ (1) be
    _____ (2) has
    _____ (3) finish
    _____ (4) dressing
    _____ (5) no error

27. Tad <u>might</u> not <u>feel</u> so guilty if he <u>honest</u> <u>explained</u> everything to Hillary.
    _____ (1) might
    _____ (2) feel
    _____ (3) honest
    _____ (4) explained
    _____ (5) no error

28. We <u>have</u> <u>visited</u> them several times <u>since</u> they <u>move</u> into the neighbor-hood.
   _____ (1) have
   _____ (2) visited
   _____ (3) since
   _____ (4) move
   _____ (5) no error

29. <u>Neither</u> the father <u>nor</u> the mother <u>want</u> to <u>talk</u> to their son.
   _____ (1) Neither
   _____ (2) nor
   _____ (3) want
   _____ (4) talk
   _____ (5) no error

30. <u>Now</u> the Democrat, <u>as well as</u> the Republican, <u>is campaigning</u> <u>serious</u>.
   _____ (1) Now
   _____ (2) as well as
   _____ (3) is campaigning
   _____ (4) serious
   _____ (5) no error

SPELLING

In each set of words, put an X next to the misspelled word. If there is no misspelled word, mark number (5).

31. _____ (1) already
   _____ (2) beginning
   _____ (3) disapprove
   _____ (4) necesary
   _____ (5) no error

32. _____ (1) leisure
   _____ (2) piece
   _____ (3) niece
   _____ (4) freind
   _____ (5) no error

33. _____ (1) governer
   _____ (2) grammar
   _____ (3) personnel
   _____ (4) superintendent
   _____ (5) no error

34. _____ (1) typewritting
   _____ (2) questionnaire
   _____ (3) planned
   _____ (4) written
   _____ (5) no error

35. _____ (1) different
   _____ (2) atheletic
   _____ (3) ninety
   _____ (4) forty
   _____ (5) no error

36. _____ (1) acheive
   _____ (2) conceive
   _____ (3) deceive
   _____ (4) receive
   _____ (5) no error

When you finish the test, compare your answers with those in *Answers and Explanations* on page 133. Then complete the chart on page 132 by checking the numbers of the questions you got wrong.

SKILL REVIEW CHART

The chart will show you which writing skills you should go back and review. Reread each problem you got wrong. Then look at the appropriate sections of the book for help in figuring out the right answers.

SKILLS	TEST QUESTIONS	STRATEGIES FOR SUCCESS
The test, like this book, focuses on the skills below.	Check (✔) the questions you got wrong.	Review what you learned in this book. Figure out why your answers are wrong.
Capitalizing Correctly	___ 1 ___ 3 ___ 2 ___ 4	See pages 22–23 STRATEGIES FOR SUCCESS ● Knowing What to Capitalize ● Knowing What NOT to Capitalize
Using Correct Punctuation	___ 5 ___ 8 ___ 6 ___ 9 ___ 7	See pages 40–41 STRATEGIES FOR SUCCESS ● Knowing Where to Punctuate
Writing Clear Sentences	___ 10 ___ 14 ___ 11 ___ 15 ___ 12 ___ 16 ___ 13	See pages 60–61 STRATEGIES FOR SUCCESS ● Writing Clear Sentences ● Correcting Non-Sentences
Using Appropriate Nouns, Pronouns, and Adjectives	___ 17 ___ 21 ___ 18 ___ 22 ___ 19 ___ 23 ___ 20	See pages 80–81 STRATEGIES FOR SUCCESS ● Using Pronouns Instead of Nouns ● Knowing When to Add Adjectives
Using Appropriate Verbs and Adverbs	___ 24 ___ 28 ___ 25 ___ 29 ___ 26 ___ 30 ___ 27	See pages 102–103 STRATEGIES FOR SUCCESS ● Using the Right Verb Form ● Adding Words to Describe Actions
Using Correct Spelling	___ 31 ___ 34 ___ 32 ___ 35 ___ 33 ___ 36	See pages 122–123 STRATEGIES FOR SUCCESS ● Spotting Spelling Problems ● Using the Dictionary

Answers and Explanations

CAPITALIZATION

1. (2) Always capitalize the word *I*.
2. (5) There is no error.
3. (4) Although months (February) are always capitalized, the word *month* is not.
4. (1) Don't capitalize words such as *of* and *a* unless they are the first or last word of the title.

PUNCTUATION

5. (4) When a sentence asks a question, end it with a question mark.
6. (5) There is no error.
7. (1) <u>You're</u> (an abbreviation for *you are*) should be used here.
8. (3) Never use an apostrophe when writing the word *hers*.
9. (1) When a sentence includes a list, put a comma after every item or name in the list except the one before *and*. (A comma before *and* is optional.)

SENTENCES

10. (4) There is no predicate in this group of words.
11. (5) All are complete sentences.
12. (1) This is a run-on sentence with unnecessary punctuation. To be correct, it should read: We expect them to approve the contract. Then we'll get our money.
13. (1) This group of words contains the subject and predicate that are needed to make the phrase into a sentence.
14. (3) The phrase becomes a sentence when <u>Because</u> is taken away.
15. (5) No change is needed.
16. (2) *Tries* matches the singular subject *he*.

NOUNS, PRONOUNS, AND ADJECTIVES

17. (1) The correct plural is *mice*.
18. (5) There is no error.
19. (3) *Him* is the correct pronoun.
20. (2) *Me* is the correct pronoun.
21. (2) The adjective *loud* should replace the adverb *loudly*.
22. (5) There is no error.
23. (4) The correct plural is *wives*.

VERBS AND ADVERBS

24. (1) The verb *seemed* matches the subject (Phil) and the time (past tense).
25. (2) The verbs *has* (present) or *had* (past) would match the singular subject (cat).
26. (3) *Finished* is the correct verb to use with the helping verb *has*.
27. (3) The adverb *honestly* should replace the adjective *honest*.
28. (4) The past-tense verb *moved* should replace *move*.
29. (3) The verb *wants* matches the part of the compound subject (mother) that is closest to the verb.
30. (4) The adverb *seriously* should replace the adjective *serious*.

SPELLING

31. (4) The correct spelling is <u>necessary</u>.
32. (4) The correct spelling is <u>friend</u>.
33. (1) The correct spelling is <u>governor</u>.
34. (1) The correct spelling is <u>typewriting</u>.
35. (2) The correct spelling is <u>athletic</u>.
36. (1) The correct spelling is <u>achieve</u>.

Glossary

Accent (page 113) The emphasis you put on one part of a word.

Adjective (page 76) A word that describes a noun or pronoun. It tells what color, what kind, how many, etc.

Adverb (page 98) A word that describes a verb, an adjective, or another adverb.

Base form (page 86) The simple form of the verb without any endings.

Capitalize (page 10) To begin with a capital letter.

Closing (page 11) A phrase that ends a letter.

Code (page 10) A system of signals.

Complete sentence (page 46) A sentence with a subject and a predicate.

Compound object (page 68) Two or more objects, usually joined by *and* or *or*.

Compound subject (page 68) Two or more subjects, usually joined by *and* or *or*.

Consonant (page 70) Any letter of the alphabet that isn't a vowel.

Content (page 29) The subject, idea, or words.

Contraction (page 36) Two words joined together to form one word.

Detail (page 33) A fact or piece of information.

Eliminate (page 74) To get rid of.

Emphasize (page 11) To make important.

Exception (page 71) Something that doesn't follow a rule.

Glossary (page 116) A list of the glosses in a book. A *gloss* is a brief explanation like the ones in the margins of this book.

Greeting (page 11) A phrase that begins a letter.

Helping verb (page 87) Verbs like *have*, *be*, and *do* that you use with other verbs to make different tenses, questions, and negative sentences.

Homonym (page 109) A word that sounds like another word. But it has a different meaning and usually a different spelling.

In alphabetical order (page 116) Arranged in the order of the letters of the alphabet (a, b, c, d, etc.).

Incomplete sentence (page 46) A group of words without a subject or a predicate.

Independent clause (page 54) A complete sentence.

Irregular verb (page 87) A verb that doesn't have the *-ed* ending in the past tense and past participle.

Object (page 66) A word used in grammar to describe a part of a sentence. An object is usually a noun or pronoun. It follows the verb.

Optional (page 33) Not necessary.

Past tense (page 52) The forms of a verb that express past time—what someone or something was like or what happened before.

Pause (page 30) To stop briefly.

Plural (page 51) More than one, for example, the word *girls*.

Possessive pronoun (page 73) A pronoun that shows possession.

Predicate (page 48) The phrase that describes the subject or that describes the action of the subject. The predicate includes the verb.

Present tense (page 51) The forms of a verb that express present time—what someone or something is like now or what is happening now.

Pronoun (page 73) A word that can replace a noun or phrase in a sentence. For example, *the Statue of Liberty* can be replaced by *it*.

Punctuation (page 28) Symbols or marks that are added to writing. They make writing clearer.

Quotation (page 37) Someone's exact words.

Regular verb (page 87) A verb that you add -ed to when you form the past tense or the past participle.

Relationship (page 18) A personal or family connection.

Repetitious (page 73) Repeated too many times.

Return address (page 19) The address a letter comes from.

Revise (page 74) To make changes or corrections.

Rhyme (page 112) Several sentences or phrases that end in the same sound.

Run-on sentence (page 54) Two or more sentences that are written together without correct punctuation.

Set off (page 32) To separate.

Sentence fragment (page 54) A group of words that is not a sentence.

Singular (page 51) Only one, for example, the word *girl*.

Specific (page 10) Exact, definite.

State (page 28) To say in words.

Subject (page 48) The person or thing that most closely relates to the verb in a sentence.

Subject-verb agreement (page 51) The form of the verb has to be correct for the subject; the verb has to agree with the subject.

Syllable (page 113) One or more letters in a word that make up a separate sound, for example, syl-la-ble.

Title (page 17) A word used before a person's name, such as *Mrs.* or *Dr.*

Verb (page 48) The word(s) that tell what someone or something is, does, or experiences.

Version (page 32) A form or copy of something.

Visualize (page 76) To see.

Vowel (page 70) One of these letters of the alphabet: *a, e, i, o,* or *u.*